GEORGE & HILLY

DATE DUE

GAYLORD   #3522PI   Printed in USA

GEORGE & HILLY

THE ANATOMY OF A RELATIONSHIP

George Gurley

GALLERY BOOKS

New York   London   Toronto   Sydney   New Delhi

Gallery Books
A Division of Simon & Schuster, Inc.
1230 Avenue of the Americas
New York, NY 10020

NOTE TO READERS
This work is a memoir. I have changed names and identifying details of
some people portrayed in this book, and a few individuals are composites.
In some instances, the precise details or timing of events have been changed
or compressed to assist with the flow of the narrative.

First Gallery Books trade paperback edition January 2012

GALLERY BOOKS and colophon are registered trademarks of
Simon & Schuster, Inc.

For information about special discounts for bulk purchases,
please contact Simon & Schuster Special Sales at 1-866-506-1949
or business@simonandschuster.com.

The Simon & Schuster Speakers Bureau can bring authors to your live event.
For more information or to book an event contact the Simon & Schuster
Speakers Bureau at 1-866-248-3049 or visit our website at
www.simonspeakers.com.

Designed by Akasha Archer

Manufactured in the United States of America

10 9 8 7 6 5 4 3 2 1

Library of Congress Cataloging-in-Publication Data is available.

ISBN 978-1-4391-6544-7
ISBN 978-1-4391-6558-4 (ebook)

To Hilly

CONTENTS

CONTENTS

GEORGE & HILLY

CHAPTER ONE

ENTER DR. SELMAN

I was nervous on the way to the doctor's office. I was besieged with second thoughts like where am I headed and why am I doing this? How did this happen? I met a girl named Hilly in a bar one night and all of a sudden I'm marching into a trap from which the only escape will be down the aisle of some church. I don't want to get *married*. Not until I'm at least sixty. Maybe if I get hit by a truck and need round-the-clock nursing care, I'll consider settling down.

As I neared the office, I was visited by Walter Mitty dreams. I saw myself hitchhiking in Bolivia, motorcycling to Chile, scuba diving under the Antarctic ice mass, bodysurfing with turtles in the Galápagos, waterskiing with crocodiles and running guns in Zambia. So many adventures lay before me. I was still in my thirties. I had wild oats to sow. Where would therapy lead me if not to a lifetime prison sentence, a ball and chain? I didn't want to have kids. Adding another George to the world's billions sounded like a crime. Above all, I didn't want to become like my compadres: those once-swaggering free spirits who'd turned into domestic robots, who'd traded in their cojones for a zero-turn lawn mower, who are awakened in the middle of the night by a screaming three-year-old instead of a purring twenty-three-year-old minx.

I'd seen the race of castrati on the Upper West Side—frail, meek, ashamed, and henpecked, the last vestige of their youthful freedom expressed by a well-worn T-shirt advertising an alternative band or fraternity scene—SONIC YOUTH; COED NAKED LACROSSE; LIQUOR UP FRONT, POKER IN THE REAR—bent under their baseball caps, pushing double-wide strollers as their battle-ax wives with linebacker shoulders babbled on about "dinner with friends." Not for me.

My pace slowed as I walked up Madison Avenue. I thought about former "girlfriends." This subject brought my riffs on freedom up short. My scorecard with pre-Hilly females wasn't good. Fond memories were few. There was the twenty-three-year-old hairstylist who turned out to be thirty-eight. The Russian girl I met on the Hampton Jitney who introduced herself as Irina, but answered to the name of Amber when someone hailed her on the street. Irina turned out to be a part-time stripper.

Or the redhead I picked up one night who said she was a graphic designer. She invited me to her apartment, played some Brian Eno songs, danced around half-naked, ordered me to whack it, disappeared into a closet, and came out in a red-rubber body suit wielding a whip. Or the barmaid with TOMMY tattooed on her lower back who said she'd come over at 5:00 a.m. if I got her a six-pack and didn't have pets. "I'm deathly allergic and I hate them," she said. "Seriously, I'll have an asthma attack and have to go to the hospital. Do you promise?" After we'd started establishing a minor rapport, I decided that it was time to bring in the cat. I figured that sooner or later they'd have to get to know each other. After ear-piercing shrieks, she (the barmaid) ran out of the apartment, screaming, "Cat lover! Pet keeper!" I never saw her again.

Cartoon Face, Froggy, Volleyball Head, Lesbian Sasquatch, Crazy, Feminem, Wolf, Snuggle Bunny, Cute Alien Head, Snow White—those were some of my failed paramours. I locked up my mountain bike on East Ninety-Sixth Street, entered the Gatsby building, and there was Hilly in the waiting room. She looked spectacular in her sundress and flip-flops. She'd come straight from the dentist and flashed her perfect teeth. All my negative thoughts vanished. Maybe it *was* time to get married. Well, engaged. No rush. One day at a time.

Another patient was sitting there, so we didn't speak. Hilly returned to her fashion magazine. I read the famous prayer displayed on the wall: *God, grant me the serenity to accept the things I cannot change, courage to change the things I can . . .* I listened to the white-noise-machine hum and stared at my devoted girlfriend. I should really count my blessings, I thought. And stop being a jackass. Now was the time to step up, get into confessional mode, and pour my guts out. Time to let Hilly know everything about me, warts and all. For her sake.

Dr. Harold W. Selman, psychiatrist, appeared and waved us in. He was a boyish, middle-aged man of medium build. Not too imposing, but solid, compact, with surprisingly muscular-looking arms. Piercing dark eyes, confident grin, steady gait. A man of obvious intelligence, too.

The consultation room featured art deco lamps, impressionistic and cubistic art, oriental vases, a ceramic monkey skull. High in one corner were seven or eight medical certificates. An open closet revealed boxes filled with antidepressants and erectile-dysfunction drugs. I felt as if I'd entered a shrine dedicated to neuroses, compulsions, and fixations.

"Can I get you anything to drink?" Dr. Selman asked as if he were hosting a social event. A dirty martini popped into Hilly's head, Johnnie Walker on the rocks into mine. But this wasn't going to be a night on the town. Dr. Selman returned from the kitchen with a selection of soda pop. An awkward moment ensued. A thread of tension passed between us. Hilly and I sat stiffly at opposite ends on a cushy chesterfield sofa, her Birkin bag and my man purse separating us like the walls of Jericho. Dr. Selman settled into his voluminous leather chair like an inscrutable shaman. Looking down on us in judgment from the wall was a framed photo of Sigmund Freud.

Dr. Selman delivered a brief introductory monologue. He'd been practicing there for twenty-five years, he said. He'd seen close to four thousand patients in that span. Addictions, ADHD, bipolar, mood disorders, anxiety disorders, panic attacks, were among the problems he addressed. His "treatment modalities" included psychopharm intervention and individual and couples therapy. Leaning back and resting his legs on an ottoman, he looked a bit weary, as if he'd been listening to neurotic New Yorkers all day. Silence. Discomfort. It seemed as if each of us were in his or her own corner, waiting for the bell.

Dr. Selman beamed an avuncular smile.

His opening gambit was a stroke of conventionality: "What brings you here?" Though we'd batted our issues back and forth ad infinitum, we were both suddenly tongue-tied. What was the matter with us, after all? What secret door were we hoping to unlock? Finally, I took a stab at it.

"I think we've had some disagreements," I said. "Nothing specific. Patterns of behavior, you might say. Me being irritable." I was afraid we were disappointing the doctor. Our problems suddenly seemed so petty, so unoriginal. I was terrified that he would find us uninteresting. "I just had an intuition that I needed to try therapy. Then Hilly volunteered to come along."

"By that I meant just wait in the lobby," Hilly clarified.

"What?" I said, dumbfounded. "That's the first time I heard you say that. I guess we'd better add *communication* to our list of problems."

"Wait," said Hilly. "That was at first. The more I thought about it, going together seemed like a really great idea."

"It's often better to approach problems on an individual basis and sort them out first before complicating matters by including another human being," Dr. Selman said. "Usually, when I see a couple, I like to meet with them individually for at least one visit to get some family history and personal backgrounds. These sessions can get pretty intimate. Coming here together may be opening Pandora's box." At first, he seemed to make an effort to divide his focus between Hilly and me, but by the third sentence I had the feeling that he was talking exclusively to her. "You may have personal issues that you're not ready to open up about. You may hear things you don't want to hear. To be hit in the face with it might be tough."

"We're in this together," we chimed. "Our lives are entwined. We can't sort out Hilly from George."

As Dr. Selman listened to us, his expression changed from curious to skeptical. He asked if a particular incident had inspired us to come.

We answered in unison, "The Big Fight."

"Sounds like Ali versus Frazier," Dr. Selman said. "Let's hear about the Big Fight."

We'd had lots of minor, bantam-weight fights. We're serial fighters. After every fight we shake hands and make up. Then one of us pushes it too far and we're at it again. The Big Fight was different. It was in a class by itself, the E Pluribus Unum Fight.

"It didn't begin with belligerence," I said. "In fact, most of our quarrels start when things seem to be going great."

I'd called Hilly at 9:00 p.m. I was lonely and needed a little love. She was beat from a marathon workday and just wanted to go to bed. But I nagged and persisted.

"Noooooooh," I whimpered into the phone that early evening in July. "Come ohhhver, I really need to seeee you. Need to talk about something you're gonna wanna hear."

"Yeah, think I'm just gonna stay home and watch *Law & Order* then go to bed," Hilly said.

"You did that last night!"

"We went out last night. Well, I met you around midnight and you probably stayed out until six."

"Four!"

"After putting me in a cab at two. And now you only want me to come over because you need some scratchy and—"

"Come onnn, you promised earlier. Been two days. You know what I'm talking about."

She was right: it had been a rough night. Truthfully, I'd gotten home at 5:30 a.m.–ish and was now pretty nicked up, suffering, and awful lonely.

"All right, but I just ordered some Frito pie from the Cowgirl," Hilly said. "Let me finish that and find an outfit for work!"

"So, eight thirty?"

"Nine thirty. Bye."

"Byyyyye."

Hilly showed up at my apartment late, but looking like a vision of beauty. I had to love her for coming. She took one look at me—long-faced, puffy, and pasty.

"Aww, you need a big basket of hugs," she said, dropping her bags in the doorway as we fell into an amorous embrace. I was instantly in a better mood after a therapeutic love tangle. Hilly looked around my bachelor sty shaking her head. Newspapers scattered everywhere, tumbleweeds of cat hair, empty jugs of grape juice, an unrolled roll of toilet paper, a big ashtray overflowing with butts, chewed Nicorette, ketchup packets, pistachio shells . . .

"Let me just clear out this area around the couch," she said. I watched nervously as Hilly hauled refuse to the kitchen, then returned with wet paper towels and disinfectant to wipe up a little cat mess on the treadmill. I should have been grateful, but I was beginning to be annoyed.

"Movie time yet?" I said.

"Wait, I have to do one last thing." Hilly peeled a dirty shirt off the floor. She waved an admonishing finger at me. "Bad boy!"

"Now. Please?"

Hilly didn't seem to hear me. Before I knew what was happening, she had set up the ironing board and plugged in the iron cord. "It hurts to see it wrinkled up like this. I got it for your birthday and it was from Paul Smith."

I went into a sulk and started tapping away at the computer. Seconds later, the air conditioner shut off with a death rattle along with all the power in half the room.

"Great," I muttered, without looking up. "Nice going. Thanks."

She heard. "Um, have you ever blown a fuse?"

"Never." Tap tap tap.

"Well, it's easily fixable. Where's the panel?"

"No idea." Tap tap tap.

"It's got to be around here somewhere."

Tap. "Hilly, it's really nice of you to clean up. I appreciate that, but you didn't have to iron the shirt. Taking it to the dry cleaner's tomorrow."

"That's why it was crumpled up in the corner?"

"I don't understand this need to always putter around and do physical work at night, all this activity and projects."

"It relaxes me. Plus I want to help you, 'cause I know you can't do these things yourself."

"You can never sit still. Need to learn how to read or take up the viola again."

"Let me check in the basement, be right back! Hope I don't see that homeless gnome lady down there or any mice."

After fiddling with the switch box, Hilly returned to cheerfully ask if that had worked.

"No! And goddammit, now my computer's turned off and I can't work!"

"Work? A minute ago you were talking about watching a movie and chewing me out for working. Oh, I have an idea!" she chirped. "Why don't you call the super?"

I scrolled through my cell phone, got his voice mail. "Carlo's on vacation for a month!" I wailed. "What are you doing to my cat?"

"Cleaning her earwax buildup," she said, holding up a blackened Q-tip.

"We've lost our power and you're fixating on earwax. And why was it so important to iron that shirt?" She tiptoed out of the room to look for help. I heard her knocking on my neighbor's door. I'd never spoken to him, but I'd seen him often enough. He was a bodybuilding freak with shirt-popping muscles. The thought of some other male coming to the rescue excited my insecurities. I ran into the hall after her.

"Get back in here right now!" I yelled. Muscles was standing in his doorway, looking back and forth between my girl and me, probably wondering if she was a victim of abuse, if he should call 911 or just put me to sleep with a love tap to the chin.

Hilly manufactured a casual chuckle. "It's nothing, really," she said. "He's just being silly and dramatic."

"You'll find the fuse box in your kitchen," said Muscleman smugly. "Every apartment in the building has one." Into the kitchen she flew. In an instant, the power was back on.

"Thanks," I muttered.

"Now I'd like a pizza," she said brightly. "With extra cheese."

I rolled my eyes, found the menu, made the call.

"Extra cheese," she whispered.

"I know!"

At last, after the extra-cheese pizza arrived twenty minutes later, we were ready for a movie: *Teddy Roosevelt: An American Lion.* But she was abstracted. The air-conditioning ordeal had exhausted her.

"Maybe you want to watch something else?" I asked. *"Pillow Talk* with Doris Day? *Gidget Goes Hawaiian?"*

"You hate that kind of stuff. I'm happy with Teddy."

"But you're not watching."

"Quiz me."

"Okay, what just happened?"

"Teddy Roosevelt was in Cuba then he became president and he used to say 'Bully!'"

"Right. But I can tell your mind is elsewhere."

"Wanna hear what happened at work today?" she blurted out. I groaned, hit the mute, and prepared to enter another dark, unmapped jungle guided by my intrepid Hilly.

"So a few months ago I was at work, and you know how we call my boss, THEO, 'the evil one'? Because she's a wicked old witch—okay, maybe she has some endearing qualities, whatever—but remember how she would only give me a half-hour lunch break so I could meet your granny Gimma at the Plaza Hotel? Well, and I never told you this—"

"Can you just say what happened without all this backstory and prologue?"

"So in front of everyone, the whole office, not just my department, some of the people from the law firm next door, Eleanor said, 'I don't know, Hilary, she's not *your* grandmother. I'm going to have to think about it.' And I said, 'I know she's not *my* grandmother—and I don't want you to take this the wrong way—'"

"Shhhh, this is taking way too long. Faster, skip to the very end of the paragraph or paragraphs and give me the punch line up front, get to the point first and then back up. And not so loud, don't have to scream, I'm right here."

"Okay, Scoopie, but don't freak out again. So I said, 'Eleanor, I know she's not my grandmother, but I'm hoping that one day she will be.' So then her eyes widened and she stared at me smiling, like she had me, and shrieked, 'You're getting married! Hilary's getting married, everyone!' But that's not what I was going to tell you. I got a gift."

"Say *present* from now on, please." It may be because my mother and grandmother dragged me to Brooks Brothers when I was a kid and forced me for hours to try on outfits that were supposed to make me look cute, but I hate clothes, I hate gifts, I hate the word *gift*. I hate the pressure to be excited, the phony suspense that's supposed to be created by the paper and the ribbons, and the way everyone stands around staring at you to see your expression of delight. It's sadistic.

"From the lawyer I told you about, with the moostash."

"Also don't like it when you call a mustache a *moostash*."

"That's how you're supposed to say it."

"Not with an overenunciated French accent."

"Whatever. So the lawyer was so happy about my phantom wedding that he gave me a magnum of champers, and I brought it with me—'"

"That's painful, too! No more talking about champers, goody bags, gift baskets, cookies, headboards, or wedd—. And I'm not one of your girl- or gay friends. So *then* what happened? Now I actually want to know."

"Nothing. I was just going to say you don't have to go to the liquor store."

"See, that's what you need to tell me up top, that I don't have to go buy you a twenty-five-dollar bottle of Sancerre. You buried the lead. Start telling your stories backwards. And. Slow. Them. Down. Maybe talk like Tonto. Now let's finish this and then we can watch something you like."

"Hilly. Want. Finish. Documentary," she said. "Then. Watch. *E.T.* Okay, grumpy kemo sabe?" She had just delivered a perfect repartee, but I wasn't about to be coaxed out of my dismal mood by her humor.

"No, you've seen *E.T.* over a hundred times," I said. "That's not healthy."

"Not. Straight. Through. One. Hundred. Times." I told her she was drinking too much. "Look who's talking," she said.

"You're driving me crazy!"

"Do you want me to go?"

"*No!* Why did you even say that? You just made it worse! Something's gone wrong with my body chemistry. My mood index is way down."

Hilly held up a copy of the French edition of *Mr. Grumpy* (*Monsieur Grincheux*), which once cheered me up. Not this time.

"Monsieur Grincheux n'est pas heureux," she said.

"We have a depressing effect on each other sometimes," I groaned.

"You make me happy. Here, I'll get you something to eat. You need your protein." Hilly reheated a slice of pizza in the toaster oven instead of the microwave. It came out tasting like sweat.

"I didn't even want pizza! And this is the worst pizza I've ever had in my entire life! You and your extra-cheese pizza!" I yelled, before pushing the plate off the coffee table onto the floor. It shattered, symbolically. We looked at each other in shock. I'd thrown tantrums before. This one seemed worse. The broken plate seemed to represent my psyche.

"I think I need to see a psychiatrist," I thought aloud.

"That's a great idea, Scoopie, and I'm really proud of you! If you want, and if it'll make it easier, I'll go with you!"

That ended my recitation. I looked at Dr. Selman—for what? Signs of hope, amusement, disgust? His penetrating look made me nervous.

"So here we are." Our time was up. I felt pretty certain I'd given the doctor enough material to convince him that I, at least, needed help. Listening to my own account of the Big Fight gave me a new perspective. I was able to stand outside myself and judge my own performance. I was able to say, "This fellow is in trouble," as if I were assessing someone else. I'm sure the doctor wondered why Hilly tolerated me. But for some reason, I felt refreshed, unburdened.

"I feel much better now than I did coming in," I said, pumping Dr. Selman's hand as the first session closed. "I'd been dreading this meeting. Now I'd like to keep talking for a few more hours. Can I ask you one more thing? We're about to go to dinner. Could you give us something to think or talk about?"

"You've said quite a bit," Dr. Selman said. "If I were you, I'd rest the subject for a few days. There might be some fallout from this session. I don't think you need to say anything until next time."

But Hilly and I couldn't stop talking. On the way out, all the way down to Seventy-Second and Madison, across the park, and over celebratory drinks at Rosa Mexicano, we babbled on. We felt exhilarated. Maybe that one session was all we needed. Maybe we'd been saved. Maybe we didn't even need therapy after all. The truth was, all we'd really done was upset the hive and let the demons out.

CHAPTER TWO

GROWING PAINS

"Growing pains," Hilly said at the beginning of the second session. "That's what it feels like we're going through. We get along really well most of the time. Maybe eighty-five percent of the time it's positive."

"We're like a pair of six-year-olds playing house," I said.

"We do get silly. When I baby-talk to him about cats, ponies, and rainbows, I think it transports him back to a safer, idyllic time in his life."

"She got me back into stuffed animals," I said. "She gave me a stuffed shark for my birthday."

"He gave me Pig, with a moving mouth, and a puppy with snowflakes embroidered on its ears. He calls me Hilly Burger, Seabiscuit, Dingbat, and the Monster."

"It's a form of affection. She calls me Scoopie."

"That's one of his cat's names. She also goes by Baba, Bobalicious, Buh-bah, Fluffy, Furball, Dopey, Scoopa, Missy Doolittle, Stinker, Sugarbush, Fatoosh, the Cat Fantastic, and Momma. He and Baba talk to each other. They meow back and forth like they're having a real conversation."

"Sometimes I interpret Baba's thoughts, emotions, various sounds, and translate," I said.

"He'll say, 'Momma, there's trouble, I'm out of Cowboy Cookout and Turkey 'n' Giblets Feast, and I need fresh water and Temptations treats, too!' Or, 'Mama, you can't just pet me for thirty seconds, get the motor running, and then stop! That's teasing. You got me purring hard enough to power the whole apartment! It's a purrrrfect storm you creeeeeaaaated!' He does it all in a high-pitched voice."

"How else are you supposed to talk to a cat?" I said in a deep voice.

Dr. Selman looked calm and sphinxlike. Still, it was hard to tell if he wanted more, so Hilly went on, "And then he says, 'Mayor Baba, did you just take some cute pills? Because you're just about the cutest little Baba girl in town. She's a goooooooooood kwaaaaaaaaality cat. We got eighteen pounds of cat here! Ohh, this kitty is sooo sweet, special, and soft—she's a show cat with a coat of many colors, and her tum tum hangs down to the floor, and when she runs, it goes to and fro, to and fro, and she likes to roll around in catnip— and we like her veryyyyy much,' which is my cue to say . . . 'Sheeee's ourrr friennnnd.'"

"Hilly doesn't always say that with enough enthusiasm."

"Well, that's because she's not my friend and she never will be. She hates my guts and all I do is spend time cleaning her dookies out of the litter box, and yet she'll never stay in the same room as me."

"Thing is, I've been with Baba for fourteen years; that's eleven before you came into the picture. She loves you, Hilly, really, she told me."

"When he cradles her, it's so sweet, like Madonna and child. Once I overheard him sing a song that goes, 'Rest, rest against the mother's breast.' Sometimes he takes his shirt off during that one, clutches her against his hairy chest."

"I don't want my shirt covered with dander because I'm allergic."

"George made up another ditty that goes, 'It's a ding-dong kitty, it's a ding-dong cat, it's a ding-dong kitty, it's a ding-dong cat!'"

"That's all I got so far."

"Then there's 'We like to brush her face, we like to brush her face, we like to brush her face—and even her nose!'"

Dr. Selman seemed more bored than entertained. I wondered what he was thinking—that we were sicker than he'd imagined, that his questions had triggered an escape mechanism that transported us back into infancy, that we were closet thumb-suckers who indulged in doll and pet fetishes and maybe even dressed up in diapers to stimulate our sexual fantasies? On occasions such as this, when diarrhea of the mouth flowed out, he would step in and hold up his hand for us to "Stop!" He reminded us that the meter was ticking, that we were running in circles. He wanted to get down to adult issues.

"Let's try to stay on some kind of track," he said. "Before we go any further, I need some background. For starters, have either of you had treatment before?"

"I feel as if I've been in therapy most of my life," I said. "After my parents got divorced when I was three, my mom enrolled at the University of Missouri–Kansas City for a graduate degree in psychology. Every semester, she'd try out a new psychological theory on me. I was her guinea pig. One semester, she fell under the spell of B. F. Skinner and started rewarding me with an M&M whenever I did something good. It didn't take me long to realize that I'd acquired a wonderful new power. I refused to do anything—brush my teeth, tie my shoes, say please or thank you—without the M&M."

According to some other fashionable theory of the times, Mom tried to demystify sex so that I wouldn't grow up with crippling hang-ups. She encouraged me to avoid euphemisms such as *weenie, willy*, and *ding-dong* and to become comfortable with calling my pecker exactly what it was, a *penis*. I had an opportunity to flaunt my liberated, grown-up attitude on the first day of preschool when the teacher asked us to put our hands in our laps and no one responded.

"Can anyone tell me what a lap is?" the teacher asked.

I raised my hand. "I don't know what my lap is, but I know what my penis is."

This response created a minor sensation in the classroom and a ripple of concern among the parents of my classmates. The notoriety pleased me.

I met my first psychologist when I was in the second grade. My homeroom teacher had become pregnant. The substitute was Mrs. Jones. For some reason, I started calling her "Mr. Jones." She'd patiently explain to me over and over that her name was *Mrs.* Jones. She should have sent me to the principal or applied a witch-hazel switch to my backside. But she made the mistake of bargaining with me. I was a fan of *Happy Days* at the time and my hero was the Fonz. So I offered her a deal. I would call her Mrs. Jones if she would call me the Fonz.

Poor Mrs. Jones agreed. When she called on me, it was no longer *George*.

"Fonz, can you tell the class what's six times eight?" she'd ask. This experience gave me the idea that I could manipulate authority figures. In spite of our deal, I kept pushing the limits. I moved my desk to a corner of the room as far away as possible from the rest of the class. Mrs. Jones acquiesced. So I initiated other disruptions.

Dr. Selman made a note on his pad. I asked for his assessment.

"Defiant," he said.

"Fair enough," I said. Perhaps to curry favor, Mrs. Jones started addressing me as Fonzie, rather than Fonz. I knew she was trying to humor me. But I considered our contract broken and went back to calling her Mr. Jones. Dr. Selman made another notation.

"What now?" I asked.

"Oppositional."

I tried to defend myself. "I was reacting to her failure to play by the rules. I'd been pretty clear about it. I was supposed to be called Fonz. All right, I admit that was pretty bad. I went on a general disruption binge. Pulling pigtails, hopping up on my desk and singing when Mrs. Jones was trying to teach."

"Exhibitionism," Dr. Selman said. I was running up the score.

"Finally, I wound up in the principal's office. The school began sending me home every day the moment I misbehaved. Some mornings I didn't make it past nine o'clock. On one occasion I just gave Mrs. Jones a funny look and in a second she was on the intercom: 'Mr. Gurley is ready to go home now!' After two weeks of this, my parents decided to send me to a child psychologist, a nice silver-haired lady with granny glasses. She was hard to read. Somewhere between strict governess and M&M's dispenser. My manipulation techniques didn't work on her. She seemed immune to both my defiance and my charm. She asked me to make a picture of my family. I got busy with my crayon and drew my mom's house and my dad's apartment at opposite ends of the paper. In the middle was a little boy in a car."

The woman praised me for the drawing but missed the

point of the rupture of what I referred to as "my" divorce. My grandmother remembers a conversation we had back then.

"Gimma, have you ever been divorced?" I said.

"You know better than that," she said. "Your grandfather and I have been married for forty years."

"It would be more better if I wasn't divorced," I said. After a long silence, according to her, I attempted to impress her with my commitment to reformation. "Gimma, I've decided I'm not going to call it a penis anymore. From now on I'm going to call it my dick."

I was in and out of headshrinkers' offices through my adolescence. By then, my father had made his contribution to my antisocial personality. He was a master of sarcasm who enjoyed making fun of people and crafting clever insults. He taught me to ridicule and mimic characters on TV—I remember his going up to the screen to tickle the double chins of contestants on game shows. He was a discontented real estate broker who was a closet poet and playwright. When I did something he disapproved of, instead of talking to me about it, he'd write a long essay and slip it under my door, thinking I'd find his musings on my defects inspirational. When he got remarried, I acquired two new siblings, a formula for friction, and all three of us spent time together under the scrutiny of counselors who tried to hammer us into a happy family. None of these experiences seemed to have worked any magic on me.

"My experience was more traditional," said Hilly. "But I was mixed up in my own way. I made my first trip to the shrink at age fourteen. My older brother, Jonathan, had been misbehaving and blamed his mischief on me. So my parents decided we should all see someone together. We lived in a small town in Ohio and the local shrink was a family friend. It was an incestuous setup. My brother and I had been at a keg party the previous weekend—thrown by Dr. Eiffart's son.

"It didn't work out. After two sessions, Jonathan and I were sent to a clinical psychologist in Cincinnati. I recognized the music playing in the waiting room and asked my dad, 'What kind of therapist plays Bartók? Does he want everyone to commit suicide?' This new shrink was a dick. He sat there in silence, waiting for my brother or me to diagnose ourselves. I resented even being there. It was unjust. I was nice, well behaved, at the top of my class. *He* was skipping school, smoking, partying, having sex with disreputable girls, swearing, and never cleaning his room. I remembered not being allowed to go to the Gene Loves Jezebel concert because my mother said I was a girl and it wouldn't be proper for me to be at a sleazy club late at night. Meanwhile, my *brother* got to go because he was a *boy*, and *he* didn't even like the band! So I finally broke the silence and said, 'I hate Jonathan.'"

That woke the shrink up. He was scandalized. "Do you know what the word *hate* means? It means you want to inflict pain, torture, or even death on someone. Is that what you want to do to Jonathan?"

"I thought it over. 'I would like to inflict pain on him,' I said. 'A little torture sounds okay. But probably not death.'"

Hilly made her second trip to a therapist when she was a freshman at Miami University. "I remember being angry and upset with everyone. I was convinced that the world was against me. I wanted to scream at the slightest provocation. The campus psychiatrist was a pleasant old woman with a thick Eastern European accent. I called her Dr. Ruth. I had a wonderful experience with her.

"She was always on my side while I'd sit there and bitch and complain about how I hated being at that school, deserved to be in Manhattan—and she would agree with me! I loved the way she made me lie down on a couch in her office, just like Freud. She never judged me. She was *always* on my side."

Dr. Ruth retired during Hilly's sophomore year. "I was devastated," she said. "I couldn't bear to take up with the colleague Dr. Ruth suggested. I knew that no one else could come close to her."

Dr. Selman didn't ask us why two people who'd had such unsatisfactory experiences in therapy would want to come back for more. It would have been a legitimate question and I'm not sure we could have answered it. I guessed he wasn't that interested in how other shrinks had failed us or how we'd outfoxed them. He was confident in his own arts and wanted to concentrate on our mission with him.

"What do you two want to get out of your sessions with me?" he asked.

"I'd like to cut back on Prozac," said Hilly. "And I'd like George to cut back on his temper tantrums."

"I guess I'm resistant to change," I said. "I want to improve. But I want to keep things between Hilly and me the way they are: the status quo."

CHAPTER THREE

A MISFIT CONNECTION

"Where do you want things to go in the relationship?" Dr. Selman asked in the next session. "How well do you two read each other? Can you intuit each other's moods and take them into consideration when you engage in conversation? Or are you always saying the wrong thing?" We'd given him a glimpse of our "communication" style, which involved fights, misunderstandings, makeups followed by more fights.

He must have been finding it hard to understand what attracted us to each other in the first place. "Why don't you tell me how you met," he said. "Maybe that will help."

It was the summer of 2001. I was in the Hog Pit, winning bigtime at the pool table, feeding bills into the jukebox, buzzed from a pitcher of Pabst Blue Ribbon, full of the confidence I lacked when I was sober. I couldn't lose that night. I was on fire. I could destroy Minnesota Fats. One after another, my defeated opponents left the pool table in disgrace.

A young woman walked by and took a seat at the opposite end of the table—shiny, full, natural-looking blond hair tumbling over her shoulders, white jeans, stunning physique, everything curvy, proportioned, soft yet tight, ideal height, well-groomed, fashion-y, and south of thirty years old. Hot and cool, too. How did I know? Because she was wearing a Judas Priest T-shirt, which signified that she wanted to party hard and have wild sex immediately. Our mutual friend Jacqui introduced us.

"So what's your favorite album by Judas Priest?" I said. I must have sounded like an interrogator because she backed away immediately. I found out later that Hilly didn't know anything about Judas except that he'd sold out Jesus Christ for thirty pieces of silver. She'd bought the T-shirt because she thought it looked badass and, whenever she wore it, guys treated her with a measure of awe.

It wasn't at all obvious, but Hilly was really a bit of a geek. She played the violin and viola. She loved the Muppets and *The Sound of Music.* Hard-core heavy-metal headbanging was not her style. But she clearly had girlfriend potential. She wasn't an emaciated, unattainable, perpetually dissatisfied, young Manhattan socialite or an ambitious, aggressive she-wolf hunting for an investment banker. I was smitten, but I'd managed with my usual verve to put her off. We chatted awkwardly for a minute. After an hour, she left without saying good-bye. I figured I'd never see her again.

"I thought he was rude," Hilly told Dr. Selman. "I was disappointed because I'd read some of his articles and thought they were pretty funny. I decided he was one of those lame, egomaniacal guys with his own self-promotional website, like Malcolm Gladwell. I thought, what a pity, what a waste."

"It's true," I said. "It looked as if I'd blown my chances out of the water before we'd even had a start. But six months later, we met again and the sparks really flew."

"You were nice that time," said Hilly.

It was well after midnight when Hilly and Jacqui walked into Siberia. I was a regular there and was guest bartending that night. She was wearing another deceptive disguise: Van Halen T-shirt, blue jeans, stiletto ankle boots, and tough-looking black leather cuff bracelets. She was stunning. Even though I was bloated and disheveled, Hilly lit up when she saw me. She'd read an article I'd written for *Vanity Fair* about Furries, a subculture whose members identify with furry, stuffed animals. She thought it was funny. Maybe there was more to me than the insolent show-off she'd met at the Hog Pit.

I made her a few vodka sodas before being ordered out from behind the bar. We exited Siberia and settled in around the corner at Bellevue, "the alcohol-abuse center of Hell's Kitchen," according to Jimmy Duff, the Herculean Hells Angels–like owner who parked his hearse right outside. We sat close to each other on a stained black couch by a bathroom strewn with refuse and chatted away. Two key events happened next. First Jacqui left and Hilly didn't follow. Then, after more babbling, Hilly just started kissing me. It was as if she couldn't take it any longer or wanted me to shut up. I became dizzy. It was a moment of pure infatuation.

"Let's start going out right now," I said. Hilly laughed, so I repeated the proposal. After a few more kisses, she began rattling off reasons why it was a bad idea. She had two cats. Her mother always said she was going to end up a crazy cat-lady spinster in a walk-up studio apartment with stacks of old *New Yorker*s.

"I have a cat," I said.

"I have psoriasis."

"I've had skin problems for years."

"I'm weird," she fired back. "I like to be alone and don't like people."

"I talk to myself and my cat."

"I'm on Prozac," she said.

"I'm sure that's a temporary thing. I've known many—"

"I've been taking it every day for six years."

My eyes wandered up and down her body. So she's bonkers. That didn't matter. I was drooling. "Let's just jump into it and see what happens," I sputtered.

"I always sabotage relationships!" she persisted. "Before they get a chance to blossom! That's how my *shrink* puts it."

"I do that, too!"

"I've never gone out with someone longer than six weeks!"

"Three weeks is my record." I told her about my failed relationships. How I'd promised myself I wouldn't get involved again with anyone until I got my act together. But I was thirty-three and ready for a real girlfriend. She must have read the subtext.

"I'm not going to have *sex* with you," she said. "It might take six months before I'm ready."

"Sex is the furthest thing from my mind," I protested. "I'm a confirmed celibate. I just want to be your friend."

"I'm seeing someone. Actually I was on a date with him earlier tonight." It was after 4:00 a.m. when Hilly agreed to let me drop her off. We kissed and fondled all the way to Charles Street. After exiting the cab, I kept my hand on the door to convey zero interest in going upstairs for a nightcap. She gave me one more kiss before lurching away. . . .

"The Hog Pit . . . Siberia . . . an alcohol-abuse center," mused Dr. Selman. "Not very propitious-sounding places to begin a romance."

"I wish I could say we met while walking our dogs in Riverside Park," I said. "Or ice-skating at Rockefeller Center, or during intermission at the Metropolitan Opera." But for me, the Hog Pit and Siberia were the perfect places for us to find each other. At the time, Siberia was a second home to me, an extension of my personality. As I came to understand, it was also an impediment to my relationship with Hilly, a rival of sorts.

I'm not sure how much insight Dr. Selman got from the story of our first encounters. He was looking at us as if we were weird, antisocial cat people, incapable of lasting relationships but somehow ready to turn a corner.

"You were both pretty intoxicated when you met and hit it off," he said. "I wonder if this was a result of emotional instability, or the direct cause of it. Either way, you clicked."

"I felt like I could connect with George, even though we were both babbling," said Hilly. "Much more than I could earlier that evening with my date. There was something cathartic in talking to George. I had his undivided attention and he responded to everything I said."

"It was powerful," I said. "We were laughing and practically finishing each other's sentences." Time was running out and Dr. Selman guided us back to the questions he'd raised at the beginning of the session. We'd just painted the portrait of a couple who had an almost supernatural rapport. But as we scratched beneath the surface of that first night, a different picture emerged.

"Sometimes she falls into silence and it makes me nervous," I said. "I'll ask her what she's thinking about. She never seems to be able to answer that question. So I dream up all sorts of things that must be the matter. One of the reasons I decided to try therapy is the suspicion that I'm not capable of having a stable relationship."

"Fighting is a regular feature of our lives," said Hilly. "It's like the only time he really listens to me is when I'm crying.

The rest of the time he has to be in control. It's like he wants me to be a geisha. He doesn't listen when I'm talking. But when *he's* telling a story, he blows up if I look at a dress in a store window."

"Because she's yawning," I said.

"I can't help that. My allergist told me that it's a reaction of my lungs to airborne pollutants."

CHAPTER FOUR

THE BOTTLE CONJURER

"Alcohol seems to be a prominent feature of your relationship," Dr. Selman said in one of our early sessions. "How much exactly do you drink?"

"Does anyone ever answer that question honestly?" I said. "I'd guess that half the time we're together, booze is in the picture."

"Ninety percent of the time," said Hilly. The truth was that our lives revolved around the bottle. It was just as strong a bond between us as sex. And it was a major source of conflict. Our drinking styles were totally different. Hilly was a sipper. But she drank every night. She was happy to stay at home, putter around, watch TV, sip and swirl. Gradually, she'd drift off into oblivion, dreaming about fluffy puppies or evil dinosaurs chasing her up escalators. Drinking was a sedative for Hilly, an energy drink for me. She wanted to relax every night; I wanted to get hammered and amped up once or twice a week. The truth about my Walter Mitty dreams was that hard drinking was the extent of my spirit of adventure.

Hilly was as picky about alcohol as she was about food.

Sancerre was her drink of choice. She disdained red wine and turned her nose up at chardonnay ("Too buttery and you can taste the calories"). She wouldn't refuse a flute of Veuve Clicquot. But it was Sancerre she craved. During one session, she referred to it as her lover.

I was an indiscriminate imbiber. Sidecars, mojitos, whiskey sours, grasshoppers, black Russians—any vile potion would do, as long as it got the job done. On an average night out I'd hit a half-dozen bars and polish off twice as many drinks. Inevitably, I'd wash up at Siberia, which usually closed around 6:00 a.m. After the front door was bolted behind me, I'd step out into the morning light. I'd look at the joggers, the dog walkers, the buttoned-down businessmen scurrying to work. And I'd pity them for all the profound experiences they'd missed getting their precious rest and dreaming of bottom lines.

If I ever felt a pang of remorse during the melancholy cab ride uptown, it was quickly dismissed by the comforting illusion that I'd just been doing my job—capturing the mood of fin de siècle Manhattan, not only for present-day readers but future historians. To serve this noble cause, I had to make the scene and interview drunk people. How could I do that without being drunk myself?

Dr. Selman appeared unimpressed by my logic. "Why not go about your business sober? The idea that alcohol enhances anyone's competence is a delusion. Isn't it possible that you're trying to narcotize your own insecurities rather than obeying some perverse variation of the Protestant work ethic?"

I laughed at his questions. "Drinks fire me up. They energize me. When I try to conduct an interview without a few drinks, it falls flat. When I'm a little wacky, it seems to put my subject more at ease. It loosens them up, too. Many of the people I talk to have been interviewed to death. They resent the same old questions and tend to give robotic answers. I try to refresh the experience, wake them up, entertain them, make them shift gears. Part of the secret is to make myself part of the interview, to arouse their curiosity about me. This throws them off guard and provokes them to say things they wouldn't say in a routine interview. Sometimes it works for me to play the buffoon, even to be a little obnoxious, to make them mad at me. I've had subjects scream things like 'You don't want me as an enemy,' 'Don't call this number ever again,' 'Please return my books to the super, and then let's never speak again,' and 'Fuck you!'

"A lot of these interviews take place in bars. What am I supposed to do, order a ginger ale?" Booze was like a tool in the tool kit, I said. It transformed me from a plodding note-taker into a journalistic magician, capable of extracting gemlike quotes from the most reticent celebrities.

I tried to impress the doctor with some of my triumphs. I'd scored one story by getting strangers to talk about vaginas and the female version of the issue "Does size matter?" Once I'd challenged liberal New York bargoers into making positive comments about George W. Bush and discovering redeeming virtues in Saddam Hussein. One evening at a black-tie event at the Waldorf-Astoria, I summoned up the nerve to corner Henry Kissinger and got him to talk about his love for Labrador retrievers. I like to think the publication of our thirty-second bowwow powwow garnered enough publicity for the Animal Medical Center (the Mayo Clinic for privileged dogs) to save a few dog lives.

"There's no way I could pull those interviews off sober," I said. Just making an appearance at watering holes such as Paddy Mcguire's, Plug Uglies, and Nancy Whiskey Pub without a glass in my hand would be like facing Wyatt Earp without a six-gun. Dr. Selman smiled but shook his head. "I cover nightlife," I cried. "Drinking's a given. It's practically a requirement. At times I depend on it."

"It sounds like an occupational hazard," the doctor said. Then he asked the question from which there was no escape. "Do you think your drinking habits would be any different if you were an insurance adjuster or a real estate appraiser or a kindergarten teacher?"

"All right. I like to drink. I enjoy being intoxicated. I agree with Frank Sinatra. I feel sorry for people who don't drink. When they wake up, that's as good as they're going to feel all day."

I told Dr. Selman about my favorite barmaid at the Village Idiot. "Natasha doesn't trust nondrinkers. She compares them to people who don't love dogs." One night, she agreed to an interview—but only if we both downed a shot of whiskey before each question. After twelve drinks, Natasha was still stone sober, all 110 pounds of her. At twice her weight, I was a slobbering basket case. She put me in a cab and took down the medallion number, lest the driver drop me off in the Hudson River.

Dr. Selman stopped me once again. We'd reached the crossroads where horsefeathers meets horseshit.

"I want to call your attention to a word you just used, *depended*. It's pretty clear you're dependent on booze. You're not in control of your drinking. Your drinking is in control of you."

I was prepared to do anything or say anything to prevent the expression *drinking problem* from entering our conversation. For that would mean that I'd have to take some action. I'd have to change, confront reality. I wanted to live in a zone of arrested time, perpetually twenty-two, perpetually irresponsible, perpetually free, and perpetually crocked.

Dr. Selman took another tack. "Why do you have to stay out so late?"

"It's a fairly recent phenomenon. In college, the bars closed at two a.m. After I graduated and moved back to New York, I was fairly responsible for a seven-year stretch. I was disciplined enough to regularly leave bars as early as twelve forty-five a.m. even if drinking bullies asked if my pussy hurt."

At thirty, I started cutting loose. The late 1990s lent themselves to cutting loose in New York. I'd achieved some minor success as a local reporter and it went to my head. I became a regular at Marylou's, a mobbed-up joint frequented by hard-partying journalists, celebrities, real and wannabe wiseguys, including a drug dealer named the Baron. That place, with its cornucopia of colorful characters and terrifying lunatics, provided me with a stream of stories. Another nice thing about Marylou's was that it always closed (for me, a less privileged patron) at 4:00 a.m. sharp, an early-bird curfew compared to the late nights that awaited me. I didn't yet know about after-hours parties.

"I still don't understand how these marathon binges are necessary to produce your stories," Dr. Selman said. "How many drinks do you consume on an average night?"

"Somewhere between eight and fourteen. But that would be over the course of eight to fourteen hours." That was supposed to make it seem like a model of healthy behavior. I appealed to Hilly for support. "It's not like I get falling-down drunk. I always have my wits about me. Right, Hilly?"

"Well, sort of," she said. "When I'm staying at his apartment and he comes back at eight a.m., he's pretty loopy. It's cute, though."

Paranoia crept in. I began to feel that Hilly and Dr. Selman were ganging up on me. I tried to shift the focus of the inquisition onto her. "Tell him about how you disappear into Hilly World every night," I said.

She responded with a narrative that made her sound like a teetotaler. "When we first starting going together, I was an assistant at *Newsweek*. So we'd carouse into the wee hours. Then I got a new job in fashion publicity and I had to get on a more normal schedule. So I had to call it quits much earlier. He'd put me into a cab around one a.m., then stay out until sunrise. When I'm getting ready for work, he's often still sleeping it off." It was true. My friends could never get over how cool Hilly was. She let me get wasted. She never complained or asked prying questions the next day.

When she landed a real, high-pressure corporate job, her wild nights were officially over. After work, she'd put in an hour at the gym, order from the lesbian barbecue restaurant down the street, watch her crime shows, then get her beauty sleep while I kept the bars afloat. But I was determined to smoke out Hilly's drinking secrets.

"By that time she was spending weekends at my place," I said. "I hardly ever had a drink at home. There was never much booze around besides light beer. Before she'd come over, I'd ask if she wanted anything. She'd act coy, as if maybe a glass of buttermilk might taste good. Then she'd allow that she just might nurse a glass of wine, if it were offered. 'Do you have anything there?' she'd ask nonchalantly. I could hear a trace of panic in her voice. 'No? Okay. No problem. There's a liquor store on Sixty-Fifth and First. Maybe another on Lexington and Sixty-Second. Sancerre would be great.' When I stopped asking her if she wanted anything to drink, Hilly began showing up with her own supplies, 'just in case' she felt like a drink. Years later, she confessed to sipping something from a Diet Coke bottle on the way uptown."

Not until Hilly later moved in with me did I realize she got buzzed every night. Four or five drinks might not sound excessive for a young career woman in Manhattan, until you factor in Hilly's weight (118-ish) and her daily ingestion of 20 to 40 milligrams of Prozac. Sometimes I felt as if I were living with a functional zombie and turning into one myself. Hilly was fine after two drinks, unless she'd had more earlier. After three, she'd yawn. Her speech slowed down. Her voice became softer yet higher pitched and dreamy. I could hear the wine in it, see it in her half-shut eyes. Her skin looked pinker, too. By the end of her third drink she was slightly out of it, there but not all there. I called this state of being Inner Hilly World. By her fourth, she was mute and borderline narcoleptic.

"What?" I'd bark.

"What-what?" she'd reply, snapping to and pretending she'd been paying attention.

"What. Is. Going. On? What are you thinking about? And not saying?"

"Nothing. Sleepy."

"You just got here, though."

"Long day. Trying to watch movie now."

"Right, but you're allowed to say something once in a while."

"Something."

"It's only midnight! Come on, you're driving me crazy! I want us to connect! Talk!"

"Okay. I have to be up in a few hours for work."

If she poured herself a topper, it was all over. Conk-out time. Finally one night, in an attempt to get on her wavelength, I had a glass of Sancerre. It was delicious, a real up drink. Soon I was drinking every day, too.

"He calls me an enabler," Hilly said. I didn't really know what the word meant, but Dr. Selman complimented her on her psychological insight. He defined *enabler* as someone who helps someone else to not function.

"Well, when she shows up with a black plastic liquor-store bag and three bottles of seltzer—"

"Well, why do you insist I come over in the first place?"

"I think this would be a good place to bring drinking back to the subject of communication," said Dr. Selman. "You drink thinking it will open you up socially and enable you to connect, but what it really does, it isolates you in your own cocoon. You both may have different drinking 'styles,' but the effect is the same. It stifles intimacy, it impairs your ability to think."

I tried to make a self-serving distinction. "Drinking at home means I'm less likely to do anything productive like reading or working."

"What do you mean by 'productive'?" said Hilly. "All you do is e-mail your high school friends about bands, sports, girls, the glorious summer of 1987."

"Right," I said. "I join you in a few drinks to be sociable and you fade off to dreamland leaving me with no one else to communicate with. What am I supposed to do for the next four hours?" I turned to Dr. Selman for support. "Sometimes after she passes out, I'm forced to go out on the town looking for someone to talk to."

"You mean that Hilly's drinking is to blame for your going out on the town and getting smashed?"

Bull's-eye. But I kept on trying to redeem myself. "I've tried to cut back our consumption by hiding bottles of vodka and pouring them down the sink. I tell her we're in a stress-free zone with zero social pressure. It's not as if we're having rowdy new friends or big-spending clients over for dinner. It's just the two of us in a cozy one-bedroom on a quiet, family-friendly block. Since all we're doing is ordering takeout, watching movies, screwing, and playing with the cat, why drink? What's the point?"

"I just want to unwind," Hilly said.

I couldn't seem to convince Dr. Selman that Hilly had a drinking problem, too. Nor did I have any luck in trying to enlist him as an ally. Never once in all our sessions did he recommend that Hilly cut back on the Sancerre. He thought it was ironic that I was posing as the moderate one, and a little outrageous of me to complain about Hilly's drinking in the light of my own debaucheries.

"Sounds like the pot calling the kettle black," he said. That encouraged Hilly to pour a little more fuel on the fire.

"He calls me Drinky, Drunky, Dingdong, Bonksy, and the Guzzler." Then she added magnanimously, "I do think it's sweet and considerate of him to be concerned about how much I drink."

I sulked. Therapy wasn't fair. Dr. Selman didn't know that she sometimes had a drink before our sessions. Of course, I didn't volunteer that I often came to the sessions with a hangover from the night before. I had to admit that Hilly was at least consistent and fairly moderate in her drinking. But it affected our time together. I tried to explain that I only wanted us to communicate better and break the routine by doing other cultural-type stuff besides watching Lifetime movies like a couple of alkies swilling Ripple in a trailer park.

Dr. Selman gave Hilly another pass and zeroed in on me. "Some people get irritable, anxious, depressed, the day after a binge. Some have panic attacks. Does that ever happen to you?"

"I admit I get the occasional headache," I said. "I admit that some of my hangovers are epic. But usually all it takes for me to bounce back is a sauna, cold-plunge pool, steam bath, massage, and wasabi to clear the sinuses."

Dr. Selman kept up the attack. "Had you been drinking the night of the Big Fight?"

We admitted to having a "coupla cocktails each," "nothing too crazy." I allowed that drinking at home in front of the television was arguably more civilized than what I did.

"If only I had the willpower to come home earlier and not get carried away," I said.

"He always says that after the fact," Hilly chimed in.

Dr. Selman delivered his verdict. "Booze is having a negative effect on your relationship. The question is, are you capable of giving up alcohol if it will improve your relationship and ability to communicate?"

"Our relationship is much more important," said Hilly. "I'd rather give up drinking than lose that. Of course, I'd rather have my cake and eat it, too." Then she made me an offer: "If you stick to a two a.m. curfew, I'll cut my drinking consumption in half." Knowing it was a pipe dream, I agreed.

After we scheduled our next session, I mentioned that we were going out to dinner. The doctor had some parental advice: "Don't drink too much."

To be safe, we decided on a restaurant a few blocks from my apartment. Hilly complained about the heat and her long day. She wanted just one glass of wine, not a whole bottle. While open to that idea, I expressed concern that when the entrée came, she'd want another, then two more at home, and we might end up doing a night on the town.

"You mean *you* will. I'll have a lemonade," she moaned to the waiter.

"No," I countered. "Let's stick with two drinks each. That's safe, that's the magic number. One bottle of Sancerre, if you have it," I said to the waiter. "Or any kind of sauvignon blanc." And in spite of our solemn vows, we reformed drinkers were tossing them down again.

CHAPTER FIVE

SIBERIA

For seven years, Siberia was my home away from home. Not the Siberia associated with penal servitude and salt mines, but the legendary dive bar in Hell's Kitchen. It was my sanctuary, the clubhouse where I could blow off steam, render myself insensate, and act like a jackass with like-minded journalists and other misfits.

My relationship with Siberia can only be understood in terms of love. Self-destructive love perhaps, but an attachment so powerful that it actually threatened my relationship with Hilly. Twice a week at least I would abandon her for a rendezvous with the "other woman." After another all-nighter, I'd drag my broken body back and promise I would never do it again—"This time I really mean it." After a few days of remorse and penance, a faint itching sensation would come over me, awakening memories and desires, and I'd find myself crawling back for more. According to my calculations, I visited Siberia at least 425 times. That translates into 3,874 Siberian drinks.

Why did I do it? Part of it was the illusion that Siberia was the secret locus of Manhattan's pulse and that I might be "missing" something if I didn't show up. I deluded myself into imagining that I might run into an important story there and that I was just doing my job. I thought that if I stayed home and went to bed early, I might lose my youthful esprit de corps. But the real reason I went was because I needed to. I couldn't help myself.

My love affair began one evening in April 2001. Drawn by rumors of a rabbit hole like no other bar in New York, I walked past the Port Authority Bus Terminal, past assorted derelicts, prostitutes snapping their fingers, a runaway shelter . . . I entered the West Fiftieth Street and Broadway station, walked down a flight of steps, turned right. There I stood beneath a bare red lightbulb above an unmarked door that looked as if it might be the entrance to some kind of storage space for Dumpsters. The ground shook from the pounding of trains rumbling nearby.

I pushed the door open and stepped inside. The plaintive refrains of "Louie Louie" boomed from a jukebox to which a beautiful girl clung as if it were her dancing partner. Three other gorgeous girls were dancing on the bar. Panties hung from exposed wires on the ceiling. The sweet, acrid smell of marijuana was in the air, along with a deafening din of conversational shouts and screams. I spotted Conan O'Brien and Chloë Sevigny in a corner. An Addams Family pinball machine seemed to be smiling at me. A man who identified himself as Pig looked me over, gave me a nod of approval, and introduced me to his sidekick, a woman with unnaturally shining eyes, the Dude. The place seemed like a benign beast that was encircling me with its giant paws and holding me in an affectionate embrace. I had a powerful conviction that this was where I belonged.

At this time in the sordid history of New York bars, Jet 19,

Lot 61, Eugene, and other pricey nightclubs with mandatory bottle service were in vogue—money-sucking parasites that fed on status seekers whose goal in life was mere admittance. Once you made it past the velvet rope, you had to part with $8 for a beer, $20 for a mixed drink, and, if you wanted to sit down, $300 for a liter of Absolut. Unless you were a celebrity, you were made to feel like a worm. Everyone was looking everyone else up and down, measuring one another's mojo, peck-sniffing, assuming looks of arrogant nonchalance, wrapped in the web of their inhibitions.

Siberia was different. It had a vibrating presence independent of the crowd. The people packed into its nine-by-twenty-foot confines weren't "clientele." They were a family of celebrants, the supporting cast. A positive voltage connected them and gave the bond of a spontaneous democracy of drinkers. As I wandered around the gyrating bodies, I was suddenly confronted by a giant, bearded man, who looked like a heavy-metal biker, a professional wrestler, or a descendant of Rasputin.

"You should have been here last night," he bellowed. "Two characters from *Saturday Night Live* rolled in late. Somebody threw a bottle against that wall. Everybody thought it was a witty thing to do. So we had about five cases of beer to keep being witty with, and we started slamming bottles against the wall until the sun came up. Then someone walked in with one hundred and fifty dollars' worth of bacon, a foot-and-a-half-tall stack of hog fat, and we made a breakfast out of it. I remember drinking a lot and eating a lot of bacon." He gave me a penetrating look as if waiting for a clever or profound reply.

"That's a lot of bacon," I said lamely.

He kept looking at me and I couldn't tell whether he was going to give me a hug or throw me out the door. All of a sudden, he let go of a roar of laughter and held out his hand. "I'm Tracy."

So I was in the presence of the notorious Tracy Westmoreland, owner—creator rather—of Siberia. For some reason, he seemed to have taken a liking to me. We sat down and he began a brooding monologue on bars.

"These other places around here—Spa, Lush, Hush, Suede, Beige, Lotus—they're nice, clean places," he said. "They're not bad places. They're just soulless. Imagine a person without a soul—how horrible would that be? Every bar in New York I've been to, every club, has no soul, has no life, no love, and they're all probably going to close in six months." He paused and ruefully shook his head.

"There are three rules here at Siberia," he continued. "No cursing, no hitting on women, and no being a meathead." Otherwise, he suggested, you could get away with almost anything there. It was your right—almost your duty—to tap into that inner, juvenile, irresponsible id and let it explode. Every night at Siberia, according to Tracy, was "a high school reunion of revelers, an after-hours in the best part of hell."

Tracy was born in Wheeling, West Virginia, and raised in Queens. His father, a truck driver and heavyweight boxing champion, did sixteen years in prison for some crime unknown to Tracy. "But they don't put you in jail for that long for no reason," he said. His mother, Carol, worked for United Airlines in the flight kitchen. After lifeguarding (and saving seventy-two lives) on Rockaway Beach, Tracy learned the bar trade as a bouncer at Studio 54's back door, the Palladium, the Tunnel, and the hottest gay club in New York City, Private Eyes. By 1991 he'd saved up enough to buy a piece of a literary watering hole in the East Village called KGB, where he got to know an old-timer who was dying of liver cancer.

"One day I show you something," Yuri kept telling Tracy. A few years went by. Then one day Yuri summoned him and led him to a closet-size space next to a stop on the 1/9 subway line. At the time, the property was a "kung fu hip-hop place" and, according to Yuri, a front for a smart crack distributor. Yuri told Tracy that it had once been a drop-off place for Russian spies during the Cold War and that the place would soon be his. It would soon become Siberia, in honor of Yuri, who was part Siberian.

Tracy told me that while fixing up his new bar in 1996, he found some old Soviet documents, passports, and rubles behind a wall, confirming Yuri's story. After the *New York Post* did a big piece on his archaeological find, it became a hangout for reporters, politicos, drag queens, and regular drunks.

Tracy finished his tale in a nostalgic mood. He was silent for a moment. Then he seemed to wake up with a start and a ritual began that I would become familiar with. First he turned down the music. Then he announced that the bar was closing. "Too many meatheads," he confided to me. "It's a purging. They're not bad people, they just don't belong. We're weeding out the riffraff; now the real party begins."

So Siberia "closed." After the purge it reopened at three thirty. Tracy and I traded a few more shots. Then he beckoned me to follow him. We went over to Bellevue, another bar he was involved in. There, he asked a barmaid in a cowboy hat to flash her breasts. The woman casually obliged him, laid herself down on the bar, and began pouring shots of Jack Daniel's into her navel.

"Don't let a drop of that spill," she warned me. I took it as an invitation and obediently sipped from that unusual vessel. Tracy was shirtless now, atop the bar, his face a mask of manic fervor. Suddenly, his legs began to churn. He ran the length of the bar, kicking glasses and bottles out of his way. When he reached the end, he dove off and, after a fairly brief hang time, fell to the earth, crashing into two guys and a girl. Somehow, no one got hurt.

The madness was infectious. I shouted for a Heineken. Tracy picked up a bottle, stepped back into the pocket, and passed it, a perfect spiral. I lunged for it but the missile was wet. It slipped from my hand and shattered.

"Another one!" I cried. Another toss, another miss. "Okay, one more!" I gave up, took a seat, rested my head on my arms. As I was dozing off, Tracy shook me. My hand was covered in blood. He put me in a cab, gave the driver $20, and said, "Lenox Hill emergency room! He's a great guy, so please don't fuck this up."

Like all good things, Siberia couldn't last. The Rockefeller Group (owned by Mitsubishi) pulled the plug, turned off the plumbing, and began eviction proceedings. Tracy put up a good fight. He stood outside the company's headquarters in Tokyo with the bar's toilet seat around his neck, a Franciscan monk and his lawyer, Tommy Shanahan, at his side. Eventually, he cut his losses and bounced back. He reopened at a space five times bigger, lacking some of the intimacy but compensating by the capacity to attract more devotees, of which I was one of the most devoted.

Whenever I heard the siren whispering in my ear, I'd react with scornful indignation. Valiant attempts to fight off the urge would follow: You don't want to do this. It's a compulsion. You're addicted to Siberia. You need to take a sabbatical, flee to a Tibetan mountaintop or move back to Kansas. The stars aren't aligned for debauchery tonight. There are more reasons *not* to go out. You have to work tomorrow. Think of your livelihood, your future.

With sober admonitions flying about my mind, I'd begin robotically to dress. I'd pace, thinking over the pros and cons:

Another thing you don't need is a two-day hangover, George. Besides, your mojo's not working, neither is your costume. Imagine what you'll look like when you wake up. There's still time to pull the chute and bail.

A flurry of text messages from Chris (friend, co-conspirator, gossip columnist, drinking bully) interrupts my meditation: "At Siberia . . . Misfits and Cro-Mags on the jukebox . . . Lots going on. Paula Froelich's birthday . . . You're drinking tonight . . . Get over here, pussy." My steely resolve begins to melt, thaw, and turns itself into a dew. The sane voice that says, "Stay home," begins to fade. I take a walk to clear my head. Testing the waters by striding down Broadway a few blocks. My pace quickens ("for exercise"). With a sudden bounce in my step I make it to Lincoln Center, down Ninth Avenue, and all the way to the corner of Fortieth.

Ten p.m.'s a little early for Siberia, too crowded, and do I really need to do this again? I stifle an urge to jump in a cab, toss my cell phone out the window, and scream. I need a little peace and quiet to think this over. I enter the falafel place, buy a beer, and duck into the men's room to meditate. I crack open the beer, take a sip, and at once I feel mellow, philosophical. Relaxing. Pretty good now. Hey, this is where things are happening in "my" New York. Might as well be honest with myself. I am already out, after all.

Back outside, I whip around the corner, break into a trot. In an instant, I'm in front of the black door that opens onto Truth. I throw it open and . . . wham! Music blaring, drinks flowing, joint jumping. Tracy at the bar, directly under toilet affixed to ceiling with a blow-up doll stuffed inside headfirst. Surrounded by rapt disciples. The mere sight of him arouses the expectation of mirth. It's always blurry in here, but I believe that's *the* Lou Dobbs doing shots and dancing with five girls by the Harley-Davidsons. Private party going on. A deejay. Socialites. Is that really Irina the Siberian model talking to Peter Beard and Heather Graham? Quentin Tarantino hanging out with nightlife queen Amy Sacco? Or am I hallucinating again? Anywhere else in this exalted company I'd be a nobody, but I'm in Siberia. Tracy summons me.

"Get over here, Gurley!" He presents me like John the Baptist to his crowd. "This is the whitest guy in New York, you're gonna love him." Tracy gives me a bear hug. "What are you drinking? You're broke again? Give him whatever he wants, Richie, he's on scholarship tonight!"

Tracy doesn't give me time to drink my drink. "Let's go across the street," he says. "I can't believe it—I'm in bankruptcy and I'm still giving away free drinks." We walk over to Cafe Andalucia for steak and sangria. I unconsciously ape Tracy's swagger. "Fuck it," he says. "We wanted to rock and roll. We wanted to have a good time. And that's why I started the bar." He makes it sound like the Declaration of Independence.

By the time we finish our third pitcher, the night is still young. Not even 1:00 a.m. Tracy holds forth on his latest projects. The new bar he's opening up to be called Dorothy's ("We're gonna let everyone *think* it's a gay bar so no meatheads come in") and his role in a "Harvey Keitel movie."

"I'm playing a down-and-out Alphabet City guy who does acid with Keitel and the two of us throw boomerangs off a roof," he says. "It's a French movie." Tracy's character is a "psycho biker–slash–child molester." He asks about my health and Hilly. The mention of her name startles me.

"Oh, that's right, I'm supposed to have dinner with her tonight." I get on the cell. Hilly's home alone watching *Law & Order*. She pretends otherwise: "No, I just came home for a second, and, sure, I can come meet you. Let me ditch these other guys." An hour later Hilly calls, sounding irritated.

"Where are you? I'm at Siberia! You told me to come here, remember?"

"I'm right here, in the bathroom!" She finds me in there with two tipsy blondes. I'll spare the details. Let's just say that a bit of fur flies. After a few abject apologies, limp excuses, and general effusive damage control, things cool down. Before long, Hilly and I are by the jukebox, arms entwined. I let her pick songs, and to make them play sooner, I reach around to press a button on the back in order to skip a few songs other patrons have selected, then waltz away like Fred Astaire. A few drinks later, Hilly and I introduce some cat-talk jive into the jukebox song lyrics.

"Take me down to the Scoopie pie city where the grass is green and the kitties are fluffy."

Suddenly, Hilly fades. "Scoopie, I think I gotta go. Have to be up in four hours."

"All right," I say. "I'll put you in a cab. Be back home no later than four!"

"Scoopie, has that ever happened?"

"It happened the time I slipped, slid off a table, and landed forehead first on the floor."

"You need to wear your bike helmet around here," Hilly says. I take her hand, lead her upstairs, and halfway up, a flying beer bottle shatters right over my head. Hilly makes a break for the door and dives into a cab.

Back inside, two pigtailed women wearing plaid skirts and T-shirts that read GO SATAN are running around and spanking people. I dance with a pale, mopey girl with jet-black hair. She resembles Snow White gone goth. When I tell her that, Mopey turns into Grumpy and drifts away. I offer her a drink.

She drifts back. We sit down. I suggest we hit Bungalow 8 or Beatrice Inn and come back here later.

"This'll still be happening," I say. "It's early. We need a break. Come on, we'll get a second wind."

"But it's three a.m. Plus you have a girlfriend." That sobering reminder sends me to the VIP room to relieve myself. Siberia's men's room is a foul sty piled high with malodorous refuse.

"Too much is just enough!" I declare. "The road to excess leads . . . no, the road *of* excess leads to . . ." I leave the VIP room in search of someone to share my insights with. I recognize a cute girl, all alone in the corner, "a wounded zebra separated from the herd," as my drinking bully-pal Ptolemy would put it. That's how I feel. I sit down and tell her we both need a companion, a co-conspirator, to get us through the rest of the night. It's a rough period emotionally, 3:00 to 6:00 a.m. Not easy fighting off those diminishing returns, keeping that buzz going, and postponing the inevitable, inexorable doom. Wounded Zebra says a vodka soda might help. I return with my ninth or tenth whiskey and a beer chaser. Oops. I go and fetch the forgotten vodka drink.

"I want you to know I'm not hitting on you," I say, cozying up to Zebra. "Just need someone to talk to right now. We really should keep an eye on each other for the next few hours. Let's see, it's three a.m. now. We have a few options. We could stay at Siberia. That'll work. Or if you want, we might go down to the Beatrice and then come back here. It'll still be raging. But a little commando mission will perk us up, give us a second wind, some oxygen in our lungs, an extra boost."

"That sounds possible," she says. "I better ask my friend though."

"Cool. The other idea—and seriously, I'm not trying to seduce you—is there's a hotel a few blocks away, a Best Western, and we could get a couple six-packs, a pack of smokes, chill out there, watch TV, relax, and just talk."

"Ummm . . ."

"I'll be honest, if it was five, ten, twenty years ago, I'd be hitting on you, trying to get you into bed. I couldn't help it because you're so beautiful and sexy. But the great thing about being forty is I don't even think that way anymore. See, I'm able to push those thoughts out of my mind, which is so liberating, so refreshing, such a relief not to be thinking about sex all the time, having *that* be priority number one. Whereas now I derive so much satisfaction from just talking, connecting with someone like you, and there aren't many people I can do that with, maybe a handful . . . and if a sexual thought even enters the picture, I can quickly, easily ignore it, zap, delete it, and, *poof,* it's gone. It makes me feel so much more in control of my life and civilized. Again, if it was three years ago, I'd be drooling right now, involuntarily, because you're so extremely pretty, it's like, what am I supposed to do? Deny reality? But it's so nice to be done with that, so important to me, and I'll never forget this moment. Do you ever want to escape, cut town, and start over? I have enough money, really, we could do it this weekend, drive a thousand miles and begin a new life somewhere."

"Okay. But what about your girlfriend."

"Oh, yeah. Want another drink?"

"Okay!" I forget to fetch the drink once more. "American Girl" is cranking, followed by "Unchained." I abandon the cute girl and start running around in circles, riding an invisible horsey. Now maybe people will understand why I'm known as Hopalong. Suddenly, I dismount, leap into the air playing air guitar, and bounce off the brick wall. A premonition: the evening is coming to a close.

Over on the stage, a half-dozen men are huddled in a strange formation. What could they be doing? Oh. Some poor soul is on his knees. Isn't Gay Night on Saturdays? I return to the VIP room. A group of stoners stream out followed by . . . a tsunami. There's a hole where the toilet used to be and now it's overflowing! No one cares. They're laughing, wading. It's like Dunkirk. Or the end of the world. The next thing I know, I'm in a cab with Tracy.

"We're gonna pass by my favorite scene of the night," he says, as the cab turns right. "I love it. On one side it says GET RIGHT WITH GOD and on the other it says SIN WILL FIND YOU OUT. It's right here, right here. Oh my God, they took it down! They took it down!" He asks the driver to stop anyway. He gets out and says good-bye. I watch him disappear into the night. Or rather the day. It's 7:00 a.m. Oh, boy, Hilly will be up and getting ready for work. I'm in the doghouse for certain. My cell phone rings.

"Where are my keys?!" she screams. "Where are you—out with some slut!" Click. I crawl home, my face green as a cabbage, a taste of roadkill already in my mouth. When I enter my apartment, it looks as if a twister hit. Clothes and pillows in disarray, coins from the change bowl scattered across the floor. I study the mess and formulate an interpretation: Hilly looking for her keys. Later she sends me an apology e-mail explaining, *Aunt Flo came to visit.*

More like Keith Moon, I respond.

The apartment still looks cleaner than it usually does, she fires back.

The keys were on the couch. I found them ten minutes after I got home.

CHAPTER SIX

THE PHARMACOTHERAPY COUPLE

Our discussions about alcohol opened the door to questions about drugs. Dr. Selman turned out to be an expert on the subject. Therapeutic use of drugs was his panacea, I feared.

"I'm taking Prozac," Hilly said. "Twenty milligrams a day. I want to cut down, but it does keep depression at bay."

"Any side effects?" Dr. Selman asked.

She looked a little embarrassed, then blurted out, "It does interfere with sex. Sometimes I have some difficulty reaching climax."

"That is one unfortunate side effect," Dr. Selman said. "How long have you been taking it?"

"I started after I got my first job, at Manolo Blahnik. I felt completely overwhelmed. But I wanted to succeed and come out on top. I looked up to my boss as a hero, but he was overbearing. Something about him, maybe his Texas accent, reminded me of my mother. She's a perfectionist. I've been trying to live up to her expectations all my life. Anyway, I couldn't sleep. I was constantly worried about work for six straight months. Then I had a mini-breakdown. It happened when two women from John Galliano's London office were waiting for me in the Manolo showroom. I was supposed to help them choose shoes for a special runway presentation. I kept breaking down and sobbing while I was trying to talk about crepe-de-chine versus grosgrain straps. The women tried to comfort me. I kept telling them I was all right. Then I'd burst into tears again. I knew I needed help. I went to see my doctor and he got me started on Prozac."

Dr. Selman asked again about side effects.

"Occasionally I get the shakes."

"Are you still depressed?"

"No, 'cause I take my 'zac every day!"

"I've tried to coax Hilly off the drug," I said. "It might be the combination of Prozac and wine, but sometimes she gets vague. She gives me a big smile, but she's not fully in the now."

"I've tried to wean myself off it or quit cold turkey a few times, but it's always been a disaster," Hilly said. "I'm pretty emotionally sensitive and need a little assistance to experience and enjoy life as much as other people do."

"What about you, George?" Dr. Selman said.

"My involvement with drugs is a little more complicated. My bedside drawer contains all kinds of stuff: Xanax, Klonopin, Adderall, Ritalin, Provigil, Nuvigil, Wellness Formula, Emergen-C, Cellular Power, chewable vitamins, fatty fish oils, Astelin, Flonase, Soma, Vicodin, codeine—"

"You're forgetting Nexium, AcipHex, Zegerid, Pepcid AC, Pepto-Bismol, Gas-X, Beano, and orange-flavored Metamucil," Hilly added. "Oh, and FiberCon."

"Sometimes I have stomach issues."

"You don't say!" Dr. Selman said, laughing. "You know, heavy drinkers often have digestive problems."

"You don't say. I also have mood problems and sleeping

problems and I'm kind of like a mad chemist, mixing these pills in an attempt to fine-tune my mind and body so I can function. I like to think of this stuff as medicine, but I also have a weakness for mushrooms, marijuana, et cetera.

"I've had bad luck with antidepressants. In the early nineties a family doctor convinced me to try Wellbutrin. He claimed it was a great drug that could cheer me up and maybe even help me quit smoking. It would take a little while to kick in, he said. After two weeks I didn't feel anything except numbness. The drug had turned me into a harmless sedated lab monkey, neither up nor down, emotionally neutered. Once in a while it made little waves and pulled hidden levers. If I got into a good mood, it would start swirling around, as if to say, 'Oh, no, you don't want that.' Then it would tamp things down a notch. And if my mood index dipped, it brought me back up a notch.

"I hated it. So the same doctor gave me BuSpar to take along with the Wellbutrin. He said it would 'bring back the highs.' I popped one BuSpar, and this time it was like a typhoon in my head. I remember sitting on a train and feeling this horrible whooshing, like an evil force. Aliens were trying to take me over. I threw the pills away. The next time I saw the doc he explained that one has to try various cocktails to see what works best. I swore I'd never again take a drug that didn't eventually go away and decided to stick with whiskey and beer."

"There are better medications than whiskey and beer," Dr. Selman said. Since I was already on intimate terms with a cornucopia of other drugs, I resisted Dr. Selman's pitch for miracle workers from his own medicine closet. He suggested I consider taking an antidrinking drug called Campral. I blew this off by referring to an article I'd read in the Sunday *Times* about "moderation management."

"It said that some problem drinkers are better off having a few drinks than none at all," I said.

That was the "philosophy" behind Campral, too, Dr. Selman replied. He went into his well-stocked closet and came back with some samples. "The only problem with this drug is that it requires taking lots of pills every day."

"That's no problem," I said. "I like taking pills." Dr. Selman seemed excited about adding Campral to my regimen. I wasn't planning to follow through, but I didn't want to annoy him or hurt his feelings. I agreed to try it out.

"Is this going to mess around with my brain chemistry?" I said.

"That's the point," said Dr. Selman.

Hmmm. I switched into my disruptive Fonzie mode. "What if I wash a Campral down with Dewar's? Would that make me violently ill?"

"No," said the doctor, unamused.

"What if I went out on a binge after I scored some kind of success?"

"Campral isn't like Antabuse, which would make you sick if you took so much as a sip of dessert wine," said Dr. Selman. "Campral would restore a chemical balance in your brain and reduce the emotional and physical shakes if you went on the wagon." We didn't get to the possible side effects (dizziness, dry mouth, gas, insomnia, itching, nausea, sweating, loss of appetite, diarrhea), which was just as well. I didn't tell him that I had no intention of ever taking this drug.

"Okay, then I'll give it a shot!" I said.

Dr. Selman persisted in his campaign to get me on one drug or another to treat my list of problems: depression, mood swings, anxiety, paranoia, sadness, grumpiness, and "irritable male syndrome." His first suggestion was Effexor and he was up-front about the possible side effects: headache, nausea, insomnia, sexual dysfunction, dry mouth, sweating, decreased appetite, abnormal ejaculation, hypertension, vivid/abnormal dreams, increased yawning, constipation, anxiety, cardiac arrhythmia, panic attacks, suicidal thoughts, homicidal thoughts, bone-marrow damage, confusion . . .

"Would it make me fatter?"

"Not necessarily."

"Would it kill my sex drive?"

"Your sex drive could be impacted," he said. "But not destroyed." I didn't like the sound of *impacted*.

Dr. Selman also promoted Chantix, an antismoking drug, and said both Hilly and I could try the mood stabilizer Lamictal. I did my best to sound interested but never took him up on either. I did accept chocolate Altoids, Viagra, and Cialis from the doctor, Vicodin and Ambien when I got a nasty case of shingles, and a "low-dosage" pill of the mood stabilizer Abilify (vomiting, uncontrollable twitching, stroke). One pill. When I was having trouble sleeping and breathing, I tried the "very sedating" Seroquel (a popular remedy for schizophrenia). For five hours it felt as if a sledgehammer were pounding my head. I was still wide-awake when Hilly was getting ready for work. My mouth was wide-open but I was unable to speak to her.

As for the antidrinking drug, I might have taken it if I hadn't called a recovering alcoholic pal who said that Campral is a last-resort, "before you go to rehab" kind of drug. Dr. Selman was clearly irked when I told him that. He seemed offended that I would give more weight to the opinion of a drunk than a professional therapist. It must have seemed to him that I was playing games.

"I wish there was a mood stabilizer that worked on you in the short term," I said. "Are there any hangover helpers?"

"The best thing would be to drink less," said Dr. Selman. "If you had high blood pressure, you probably wouldn't balk at taking medication to lower it, right?"

"Right. But by being constantly even-keeled, wouldn't I lose a sense of spontaneity?"

"You mean, would you be less impulsive? Probably. Effexor is a really great drug, and that's what I or practically any psychiatrist would recommend at this point. Based on what you've been telling me, George. Based on your many symptoms."

Sometimes Hilly would be all in favor of antidepressants. "Get him on something now!" she said at the beginning of one session. But more often than not she was as against the idea as I was. She worried that I'd become more depressed, especially if I became fatter and less horny.

"Not everyone gets those side effects," Dr. Selman said. I felt like his office was a drug emporium. This bothered me. It seemed counterproductive to someone who already tended to take pills for everything. More than once, I thought I should go down another path, the one Hilly recommended—multiple laps in the swimming pool and a long vacation from pills. Second thoughts always entered the picture whenever Dr. Selman disappeared into his closet to rummage around for a new sample pack for me.

"I don't know, I'm pretty used to depression," I once said. "It's so familiar that it's comforting in a way. Depression makes sense. It's realism."

"The other day it was pouring rain, just miserable outside, and for the first time in weeks, George had a great big smile on his face," Hilly said. "I've never seen him so happy."

"Exactly! And I actually like the mood swings. Really, I'll do anything to avoid taking these drugs."

"You're already taking drugs!" Dr. Selman cried.

"Well, anything to avoid taking those particular drugs. Now if you were going to offer me Demerol once a month . . ."

"I'd be in favor of something that would keep him away from those paralyzing, catatonic states he gets into when he curls up on the couch in the fetal position," said Hilly.

"Will I still be able to get melancholy once in a while?" I asked.

"So do you want to try taking medication or not?" Dr. Selman said with obvious annoyance.

"I think I'd rather keep being miserable," I said. "But seriously, are you at all optimistic about us? Is there any hope for my redemption?"

"This is not a church," he said.

CHAPTER SEVEN

WRESTLING WITH THE DOC, ROUND ONE

"Not a bad line," I said to Hilly on the way out. "A nice way to end the session. But the way he said it? That hurt. Not a trace of humor, right?"

We were both frustrated with Dr. Selman's refusal to map out a strategy. We felt that we'd made his job easier by spilling out our guts, and now we wanted some payback, not to mention some reassurance that we weren't certifiably doomed. He seemed noncommittal and ambivalent. If anything, he seemed partial to Hilly and judgmental of me.

The imp of paranoia possessed me. I concluded that Dr. Selman had fallen in love with Hilly and wanted to steal her from me.

"Maybe you're being overly analytical," she said. "And don't be so hard on yourself."

"Fine, I'm paranoid. But I think I'm right. Even paranoids have enemies."

Discussion of such serious matters called for cocktails. Over dinner and drinks at Shun Lee, we agreed to confront Dr. Selman at the start of the next session, and if we left feeling depressed, we'd find another shrink. Or forget headshrinking altogether.

We were both nervous as the session began, fearful that confrontation would get us booted out of the doctor's office.

"Should I start, Hilly?" She nodded. "I just want to say that I felt you were pretty hard on me last time," I said. "It upset me. I felt as if I'd been sent to the principal's office again."

"Why?" he asked gently, yet poker-faced. "Tell me what made you feel that way?"

"Well, your harsh, disapproving attitude. I want to give you the benefit of the doubt. Maybe this is all part of a 'tough love' technique to get us to figure things out on our own a little. . . ."

"Go on. Anything else?"

"Well, then you were kind of looking at me like you weren't exactly amused. Was this paranoia on my part?" For the first time since we'd met him, Dr. Selman laughed. It felt good and reassuring. I had a mood upswing. He likes me after all. He finds us charming and amusing. Not so fast.

"What about you, Hilly?" he said. "Do you have anything to say?"

"I guess I need some feedback and positive reinforcement, too, from time to time."

"Why do you think you need those things from me?"

"You seemed a little down on us last time, and, you know, negative."

Again he laughed. "What was negative about our last session, exactly?"

"Well, when you said, 'This is not a church,' it came out

funny but also kind of cross," she said. "I respect your serious-
ness. I understand this is not an inspirational, self-help, feel-
good-type situation. I know we're not here for warm fuzzies
and we don't want a life coach or a cheerleader. But I'd like to
know more about your style, your approach, your philosophy
before we . . ." Her voice trailed off. She didn't want to mention that we'd considered terminating him.

His technique, which had something to do with us figur-
ing things out for ourselves, would remain a mystery for the
next three years. I'd end up telling him that he was really good
and masterful, that he had some kind of genius in moving us
forward without seeming to. But back then, everything was
murky. We didn't seem to be getting anywhere. The only thing
that was clear was that there wasn't going to be any quick fix.
Dr. Selman did occasionally drop a few hints and tidbits to
nudge us along in the direction of enlightenment. For example, he allowed that past experiences tend to color present-day
relationships, and that people often repeat the same patterns
throughout their lives. While it was his job to point out some
of these patterns, he was reluctant to dwell on them if he
thought our revelations were extraneous, disruptive, or de-
structive to our already shaky status as a couple.

"But I still think if some past experience is weighing on
my mind and still fresh decades later, then wouldn't that be
relevant?" I said.

"I don't want to pour cold water on any insights you have
about your childhood," he said. "But that's the kind of thing
for individual therapy. I'd still encourage you to consider that."
Sure. Great, I thought, now this is going to cost $800 a week.
Soon I'll be broke and even more screwed up.

"We want an ongoing diagnosis," Hilly said. "We want
to chart our progress toward better communication. And it

would also be nice to get some supportive thoughts, a pep talk at the end of every session." Then she made a sudden detour that piqued Dr. Selman's interest.

"I'd really appreciate it if George would stop criticizing me for saying *like* a lot. It's like he's judging me, morally. And for him to stop telling me to 'cut to the chase!' and 'stop burying the lead' every time I tell a story. And he's always badgering me to read the *New York Times* every day. 'It's a must-read!' He's forever giving me orders: 'Pick up Baba, play with Baba, pet Bobbie.' It never ends. And any time he can't get hold of me, he'll leave a thousand messages demanding to know my whereabouts. This usually happens when he's been out late the night before. God knows where *he's* been."

"Wow," I said. "May I address these one by one?"

"Well, you can. But you're incredibly controlling in general! A control *freak*."

"Am I really that bad? How controlling on a scale of one to ten, ten being the worst?"

"Nine." I wasn't prepared for this. I thought we'd made a pact to go after Dr. Selman, not each other. The rest of the session didn't go well for me. The conversation centered on my controlling nature and irritability.

"So where do you two think this is all heading?" Dr. Selman asked as we headed for the door. It sounded rhetorical, as if our situation spoke for itself, as if the answer were something like "Nowhere, fast."

CHAPTER EIGHT

D.C. PANDA

Hilly had been trying to persuade me to travel with her to Hawaii for Christmas. It was a dream of hers. She'd found a special deal with Delta, a round-trip fare that wouldn't cost us any more than a trip to Peoria. She'd already bought her ticket and planned to meet her parents there. I should have been touched by her desire to wallow in paradise with me, but the thought of planning that far ahead filled me with unholy terror.

We had often discussed my phobia for planning with Dr. Selman. I told him that I'd rather decide a week before and pay ten times as much to go to Hawaii than save a fortune and make a commitment in the here and now. Planning made me feel claustrophobic, trapped. I couldn't handle the details. In the end, I refused to go.

I tried to romanticize my behavior as a youthful refusal to become a dull, circumscribed, programmed adult. I told Dr. Selman that I wanted everything in my life to remain as unpredictable and chaotic as it was when I was in college.

I wanted my apartment to be a bomb site the way it was in the eighties. I wanted to be spontaneous, unprofessional, and somewhat weird. Dr. Selman suggested that I was giving a self-serving spin to mere laziness and a childish desire to avoid responsibility.

Against this background, Hilly's proposal to go panda-hunting rose up and stirred my sense of guilt for having let her down on the Hawaiian junket. For months she'd been talking, Can't we go see the little panda baby? What about the baby? Panda, panda, panda. Baby, baby, baby. Panda baby! Tai Shan this, Tai Shan that.

It was beginning to get on my nerves. It felt like an ultimatum to make up for my failure to perform the holiday rituals. She kept mentioning how I hadn't spread enough joy on Christmas. I hadn't even been with her on New Year's Eve. Her birthday was coming up, as was our fourth anniversary. The pressure overwhelmed me. I caved and agreed to drag myself to D.C. to pay homage to cute, cuddly, little Tai Shan. I thought I could overcome the inanity of this venture by making it a personal pilgrimage to the nation's capital, an opportunity to put my wayward life into the perspective of great epic American themes: the discovery of the New World, the taming of the wilderness, the emancipation of the slaves, the defeat of totalitarianism, Life, Liberty, the Pursuit of Happiness, etc.

Penn Station was like a refugee camp when we arrived. All departures and arrivals were hours late. When I learned that a train was stuck in the tunnel, my hopes soared. Maybe I wouldn't have to go. Yet I'd get credit for agreeing to go. It was too good to be true, of course. Before long, she and I were standing before the schedule board. With grim, mechanical inevitability, our departure time rolled into view. Hilly literally jumped up and down.

"Scoopie," she cried. "We're going to have so much fun! Isn't this exciting!" True to my killjoy self, I hushed her and asked her not to call me Scoopie in public. But she couldn't master her excitement. She was beaming, ebullient. "What do you think Tai Shan is doing right now?" she wanted to know.

My own thoughts were on visions of Old Glory, the dawn's early light, amber waves of grain, unconquerable yeomen throwing off the chains of tyranny. I was huddling with my brothers-in-arms around the campfires of Valley Forge. I was marching with a million other protesters, fighting injustice at the same time I conquered my personal demons. In one ear I heard heroic voices delivering immortal words, in another Hilly's incessant panda-bear baby talk. It created cognitive dissonance: "Fourscore and iddy-bitty years ago . . . our ga-ga, goo-goo fathers brought forth upon this teeny-weeny continent the cutest little baby panda bear you ever did see."

"We're going to our nation's capital!" Hilly shrieked.

"And I'm going to the bar car," I muttered. Somewhere near Philadelphia, after three Amstel Lights, I got in a better mood. By the time we arrived at Union Station, I was able to make a resolution: I would try to be civil.

The cab dropped us at the Hay-Adams Hotel, across the street from the White House, where we'd booked a room that cost $400 a night. Hilly called out a greeting to "Dubya" and waved. After she'd inventoried the free bath products and the minibar in our room, she pronounced the hotel "the best place in the world." She threw open the curtain and cried another hysterical greeting to the president of the United States.

After a room-service dinner, we had more drinks in the basement bar, Off the Record. Hilly was euphoric. She chatted up a retired air force man, a public relations man, and a libertarian who delivered an endless monologue about the increased security since 9/11. At midnight or so we returned to our room for nightcaps, and after a few pleasantries we were tangled in each other's arms.

"Stop looking at the mirror!" she said.

"I'm not!"

"You are, too! It's embarrassing, I'm fat!"

"No, you're perfect! You look great!"

"I'll stop if you do it one more time!"

I slept like a baby for three hours and woke up at 6:45 a.m. The fun-killing side of my personality returned.

"Close the curtains," I growled. "What's wrong with you? Why'd you turn the lights on?"

"It's the sun."

"I can see that, it's awful. Get rid of it. Why'd you have to wake me up so early?"

"It's my birthday!"

I meant to say *I think you're mistaken*, but it came out "I think you're a mistake." Silence. I opened my eyes to see if she was crying. Not yet. I tried to get back to sleep, but couldn't. Given my aptitude for hurting her feelings, the misunderstanding was understandable. After a few minutes I attempted to explain.

"I meant I think you might have *made* a mistake," I said. "Because your birthday's over, it was yesterday. Now can you be quiet for one second?" Hilly sulked for a moment, but her irrepressible manic enthusiasm soon won out.

"Get up, Scoopie! You promised to be nice. Have some breakfast now like a big boy." She was lapsing into her mode of babying me. I could feel the spleen percolating up. In the bathroom, I examined the contents of my toilet kit, saw the samples of the antidepressant Dr. Selman had been urging me to take. I mixed ten milligrams of Ritalin, fatty fish oils, and mango-flavored marijuana. After a half-hour shower I was a different person, ready to face the day, ready to be a good little boy. In the taxi, I apologized for the "mistake" remark.

"I don't want to replay this morning," Hilly said. Then she commenced to replay it. "You were really *mean*. You yelled and screamed! There's the Mayflower Hotel, where Monica Lewinsky showed her big bottom."

"Wasn't that in the Oval Office?"

"She showed her big bottom everywhere."

"Well, she got a bum rap," I said, laughing richly. Hilly rewarded my witticism with a fainthearted chuckle. "I'm serious, I like her. She was cool to me once. Shy. Quiet."

"Let's drop it. It's my birthday." At a light a van pulled up alongside us and its dreadlocked driver began to serenade Hilly.

"I'm like Ray Charles dawg, I don't see none of y'all!" he sang. We laughed and so did he. My mood perked up. At the zoo, we passed an emu, some elephants, some mountainous elephant dung. Then we followed a group of middle-aged women who claimed to know where Tai Shan was. Ahead we saw a crowd huddled together, pressing up against a railing, pointing their cameras. It was a false alarm. Mama and Papa bear were there. Not Tai Shan.

"What, do we have to stand here and wait?" I asked. "How long is this going to take?"

"He's right below us," said a woman, staring straight ahead. An uproar of oohs and aahs greeted the little superstar when he finally condescended to appear. Everyone started clicking away, giggling, clucking, going "Awwwww!" Hilly fell into an ecstatic trance.

"Oh, oh, *oh!*" she cried. "Oh-oh-oh-oh-oh-oh. Ohhhhhh. Oh-ho, hello! Oh-ho-ho-ho. He is soooo cute."

"You should see him run," said the same lady, obviously a Tai Shan groupie. "He just sort of waddles when he runs."

Hilly cackled. A delirium possessed her when he struggled over a rock and up a hill. "You can do it, Tai Shan!" she cheered. "Ohhh-ohhh." The bear-doll waddled into his mother's arms. "Do they ever all cuddle up together?" Hilly asked her new friend. "Really? What's he eating?"

"He's chomping on some bark. Sometimes he chews on his toes."

"Oh-ho-ho-ha-ha-ha-ha! Ohhhhhh. Oh-ho! Oh-ho-ho-ho. Hee-hee-hee-hee, he is so cute!"

I felt isolated, like an agnostic caught in an orgy of religious nuts. In an attempt to gain access to her enraptured psyche, I asked Hilly what she'd like to do with Tai Shan.

"I want to scoop him up. Cradle him. Rock him back and forth," she said, transfixed. "Play with him. Brush him. He's only a little baby after all. I want to cradle him! He just wants to be with his mama. He just wants to be hugged. What a little angel. How much do you think he weighs?"

"Thirty pounds," said the lady.

"No way! That's what I weighed when I was one year old," I said.

"Oh, look at his little feet. Scoopie, how many pandas are there in the world?" Hilly said. "If they can clone cats, why can't they clone pandas? We should breed mini-pandas! We'd make millions of dollars. Aww, he's just like a *baby*. He's a little Scoopie!"

Someone said that Lynne Cheney had been allowed to pet Tai Shan. "It's not fair," said Hilly. At last she became aware of me. "Can't you do something? Can't you say you're a journalist? I want to pet him, too."

I tried to explain to her that my powers were limited. I told her we had a full day of sightseeing ahead of us. With infinite patience, I managed to lure her away from the insolent, egocentric, overrated little bear.

At some point, it dawned on me that the D.C. trip had a hidden agenda. Tai Shan was a surrogate for Hilly's longing to have a baby. That was why she doted on pictures of me in babyhood, why she talked baby talk to me. The D.C. trip was designed to show me what a good mother she would be. The subtext was marriage. I was caught in a pincer move. Suddenly I understood that the "bam-bam" earlier was really a trap. A ditty played through my mind: "Love and marriage . . . go together like a horse and carriage. . . ."

A familiar dread came over me—the dread of playing house, making babies, changing diapers. I was going to turn out just like my domesticated, neutered friends. I had a vision of playpens filled with plastic toys and Gerber baby food smeared across the kitchen floor. I heard the shrill cry of a colicky infant and his mother repeating idiotic nursery rhymes. I had to attempt a breakout maneuver. I wanted to flee.

I thought a tour of the White House might bring Hilly back to a rational, human, adult perspective, but even there her animal fetish found material for excitement and hurt feelings. Her chief interest in that Grand Central station of world power was the Bushes' two Scotties. She wanted to see them. She wanted to play with them, to see if she could make them roll over and play dead. She sat down on a bench and sulked.

I tried to console her. "I asked one of the Secret Service people if the dogs are let outside to play, and they said no." She was disappointed no Barney toys were in the gift shop, and I said, "If it takes all day, we'll find one for you."

Hilly perked up. "If you had to choose one, would it be Barney or Miss Beazley?"

I tried to distract her. "I didn't like it when the guide pointed out the sniper on the roof."

Hilly gamely played along. "I was actually really scared, too. I thought he was aiming at us."

"They're ninety-four percent accurate from a thousand yards away." I told her that I had a sense of sympathetic connection with Lincoln and Kennedy. Integrating my own personality into the context of American history was part of my D.C. mission, I explained. She didn't seem to get it. "Are you still mad at me or something?" I said.

"Of course not, Scoopie! All the presidential portraits . . ."

"It's like you can sense their presence," I chimed in. "It makes me feel like this is a good country." Now we were cooking.

"It is a good country and we have a good president!" she cried. "People take him for granted."

"Clinton really shouldn't have done all that stuff with Monica in the Oval Office," I said emphatically.

"It was a disgrace." She seemed content with that judgment, but then her innate sense of compassion reasserted itself. "But not too many people could handle eight years in there without a little stress release." So much for brooding on great themes. Hilly looked around the White House grounds.

"Everything is so pretty, well designed, and manicured," she said. Suddenly, I became aware of how deserted the nation's capital seemed. Only tourists and religious groups were on that street. Where were the armies of technocrats and the limousines bearing politicians to their mischievous toils?

We drifted on to the aquarium, back to the world of nature and animals that were oblivious to filibusters, earmarks, and the other levers and gears of governance. But the wild kingdom disappointed us, too. The shark was three feet long, max.

On to the Smithsonian we marched. At the National Museum of American History, we got into the race-car-simulator ride, fastened our belts, and began jerking side to side and flipping over.

"Ohhhhhhhhhh! Whoooooo, ha-ha!"

"Whoa-ho-ho-ho-whoaaaaaahhhh! Oh my God! Ohhhhhhh. Ha-ha-ha! Wow!"

It was a weird parody of pandamania, a mechanical-induced ecstasy. It actually gave my spirits and digestive tract a boost. I thought perhaps that if I could start off the day in the machine, I'd be less cranky. I made a mental note to take this up with Dr. Selman and ask him if agitation therapy had any validity. But the positive effect lasted only a couple of minutes and I began to experience a paranoia induced by crowds, security guards, and the oppressive bombardment of xenophobic images—omnipresent star-spangled banners, PROUD TO BE AN AMERICAN printed on boxer shorts, mouse pads, shot glasses, all those buttons and souvenirs. So much presidential and first-lady junk.

"It's really freaking me out!" I cried.

Hilly held my hand and tried to comfort me. "I can filter out everything that's not related to Jackie O."

"What? Why? What on earth are you talking about?"

"She was such a strong woman. So much grace, so much composure, and so much class, and *sooo* much style. She's an inspiration. I can't wait to read my two new Jackie O books."

"No, why are you telling me this? I have to get out of here right now!"

"Sorry, I just wanted a stuffed Scottie dog. I thought you liked the Archie Bunker chair. Did you know that FDR had a Scottie, too?"

"No, no, no!" I cried. "Let's get out of here." Marijuana

paranoia was stealing up on me. Planes were flying close to the Washington Monument. It occurred to me that one could easily turn at the last second and crash right into the iconic obelisk. Was that another thing we'd stolen from Egypt? No wonder religious radicals want to destroy us. Fighter jets were probably circling thirty thousand feet up that would stop the plane before it tried anything like that, but we were vulnerable, helpless. We were probably surrounded by terrorists. We'd foolishly put ourselves right in the bull's-eye.

"Let's keep moving," I said. We really need to send a message to these people who want to obliterate us, I thought. *Don't mess with us.* This Homeland Security business is a joke. We were being pursued by terrorists dressed up as joggers. They kept running up from behind us—in pairs. "Here comes another one! Hurry, faster, faster! Oh, your cell phone's ringing, multitask! I'm never coming here again."

My growing panic triggered Hilly's alert mechanism. "Scoo-peeee! Positive attitude."

"Well, I'm not going through one more security check. It's like a police state here."

Back at the hotel we watched *March of the Penguins,* seeking refuge in the world of non-neurotic birds. I fell into a peaceful sleep, until Hilly started playing with her Barney doll.

"Put him down and pay attention!" I snapped. "Those male penguins stay like that in a circle for months and protect the babies until their mamas come back to regurgitate into their mouths." Later, Hilly drew me a bubble bath, then we got ready for dinner.

"You look like Paris Hilton with your hair like that," I said.

"Oh, gee. Thanks."

"I meant it as a compliment." After a good steak dinner, I wanted a second bubble bath. While the water was running,

Hilly ordered a bottle from room service. When it arrived, I scolded her, "I don't even like champagne. It gives me acid reflux."

"It's my birthday!"

"But you did it on the sly. You tricked me."

"Sorry."

"I am, too." We kissed.

She pulled away. "You haven't brushed your teeth since we got here. Gross!"

"Shhhhh! I forgot my toothbrush and I've been swigging Listerine."

"It's still gross. Chemical smelling."

"So have I ruined the weekend?"

"No, not at all. I was really expecting you to throw in the towel right before we went to dinner. Thanks for being such a good sport."

"You liked the sweater I got you?"

"I *love* it. Love, love, *love* it."

"Don't go overboard."

The gentle sway of the train and the rhythmic sound of the iron wheels rocked me into a peaceful sleep on the way home. But my dreams were troubled by grotesque images: my son, my firstborn and heir, George Hammond Gurley IV, appeared as a monstrous hybrid, half-human, half-panda, cuddly but rabid and infested with lice. . . . The White House appeared to me as an animated, talking cartoon speaking like Donald Duck: "Fourscore and itsy-bitsy years ago, our goo-go, ga-ga fathers brought forth upon this kootchy-koo continent . . ." George Washington showed up in a panda suit wielding an ax and proclaiming, "Father, I cannot tell a lie." In the background was Hilly's singsong voice: "Tai Shan, Tai Shan, baby, panda, panda baby, baby, baby, baby, panda, panda, panda . . ."

CHAPTER NINE

ENTER TAMMY

One of the things that impeded our progress in therapy was my occasional attempt to turn our sessions into a sitcom. Part of me wanted to tell stories and entertain Dr. Selman. The other part genuinely wanted help. The two were in conflict.

For laughs, I brought up the mirror in the D.C. hotel room. But it also related to the fantasy/reality dichotomy in my life. I was anxious to review my sexual history with Dr. Selman because I thought it might provide insights to my personality problems and my relationship with Hilly. But he usually brushed me off, questioning its relevance or suggesting that this would be a matter for individual therapy. I suspect that was in part because he was wise to my disruptive ways.

"George keeps slipping into these catatonic states," said Hilly the next time we saw Dr. Selman. "Sometimes he just stares into space." She was right. My trances were an escape mechanism. We'd been spending so much time together, I was feeling trapped. I wasn't used to that much intimacy.

"I used to seek refuge in *erotic* daydreams," I said, trying to get a rise out of the doc and provoke Hilly. "I'd conjure up a pair of legs I'd seen crossing Park Avenue, a long mane of golden hair on the head of a receptionist at the dermatologist's office, two luscious lips and a pair of magnificent boobs etched in my memory from a *Oui* magazine I kept under my bed when I was twelve years old, and then put the parts together into a superhot Frankenstein-monster composite. Then I'd insert myself into the picture." Dr. Selman said nothing. He may have picked up that I was being weird and provocative. Hilly looked over at me in disgust. "Just kidding," I whispered. "It's the kind of thing Ptolemy says all the time."

"Who's Tolomy?" Dr. Selman asked.

"He's a real piece of work. A real charmer. A very bad influence. But other than that, he's a great guy."

"Hilly gets into trances, too," I said.

"And it upsets you when I do."

I tried to change the subject and appear upbeat. "We had more highs than lows on the D.C. trip."

Hilly perked up. "It was exciting. It was so easy to get him out of bed. He was actually willing to go out and do things."

Dr. Selman expressed concern about my trances. I tried to make light of them.

"We rode a race-car simulator," I said. "It turns you upside down and flips you around. I felt better afterward. Is it possible that the agitation rejiggered my body chemistry?"

Dr. Selman frowned.

"Sex has the same effect on my downers," I added. "By the way, our sex life has improved recently."

"What do you attribute that to?" asked Dr. Selman. "And what was this about a mirror?"

"They had a mirror on the wall of the hotel room in D.C.," I said. "Do you think that's a normal, healthy thing?"

"It sounds normal to me," said Dr. Selman.

"I'm worried that there's something kinky about it. Isn't there a danger that if you start down that road . . . maybe you can't do it without a mirror?"

"It's easy enough to get a mirror," said Dr. Selman.

"But what if you get more turned on by the image in the mirror than . . ."

"Well, who are you looking at?" said Hilly. "Yourself? And no way are you putting one on your bedroom ceiling."

"A few times I couldn't help focusing on the image rather than us," I said. "Who knows? Maybe that stems from *Charlie's Angels*, or having a subscription to *Playboy* when I was in fifth grade, and more recently friends forwarding me clips from terrible websites like exploitedbabysitters.com. Or could it be that sometimes I feel isolated when we're having sex? As if only part of me or us is there? What if sometimes I'm more turned on by fantasy than reality, or Hilly's thinking about Antony Langdon from the band Spacehog, whom she used to date?"

"Fantasy is part of everyone's sex life," said Dr. Selman.

"But what if you can't perform without a fantasy? What if you start preferring fantasy to reality?"

"Don't be so dramatic," said Hilly.

"My theory is that the mirror was *right* there and I couldn't help myself," I said, blaming the Hay-Adams. Next, I begged Dr. Selman to let me tell him about my first sexual experience. He didn't look too excited by the prospect, probably anticipating a farcical digression, but his silence inspired me to plunge ahead.

"I was just seven years old."

That got his attention. "Isn't that a little young?"

I'd opened the door. I began the tale of my childhood seductress.

"Tammy was my next-door neighbor, and in second grade. We hit it off from the moment we met. We made a tin-can telephone so we could communicate between our bedrooms. We wrote GEORGE LOVES TAMMY 7 DAYS A WEEK and TAMMY LOVES GEORGE ON SATURDAYS AND SUNDAYS in crayon on my bedroom-closet wall." But Tammy wanted to move the relationship into less innocent waters. One day, when her parents were gone, she shut her bedroom door and suggested a new game for us to play.

"No one will ever know," she said. Before I could even consider flight, she pulled down her pants and introduced me to the startling differences between male and female anatomy. "Now it's your turn," she said. Down came my drawers. She beckoned me to come closer and we actually engaged in a kiddie version of intercourse.

"Where were your parents?" asked Dr. Selman. In fact, the next time we were engaged in our mischief, my mother opened the door and caught us.

"Mom was smiling," I said. "She looked amused." But Tammy panicked. She zipped up her cutoff jeans and ran home. Mom assured me that what we'd done was natural, nothing to be ashamed of. It was something adults did to make babies and to make themselves feel good. But I didn't buy into Mom's reassurances. She put an end to the affair by telling Tammy's parents.

"I knew there was something 'wrong' about what Tammy and I had done," I said. "The thing was that I didn't feel guilty about it. To me, the transgressive aspect was part of its appeal. Doesn't that tell us something?" I thought it had to be a key to my personality.

Dr. Selman spared a faint smile. He might even have been a little impressed. But instead of offering some clairvoyant interpretation of my tale, he turned to Hilly. "What do you make of all this?"

"The first time I heard the story, I didn't believe it," she said. "Now I think it's strangely sweet because I remind him of this little girl."

"There has to be *something* a little weird about that," I said. "Right? What if I were to conjure Tammy up when Hilly and I are having sex? Would that be normal?"

"I think I remind him of an eight-year-old girl because that's about my emotional maturity level," said Hilly with a laugh.

"Do you ever envision me as a little boy when we're having sex?" I said.

She didn't think that was funny. "My obsession with you as a little boy has nothing to do with me wanting a baby. It has to do with the fact that you were the most adorable and plump angel baby in the entire universe, and you had great big wedges in between the fat that separated your knees from your calves! I have a collage of photos of George when he was a little baby. Whenever I'm mad at him, I look at it and it cheers me up. He was so sweet, and if I were to ever have a baby, I'd want one just like him."

Since I'd forced Tammy into the session, Dr. Selman asked Hilly for feedback on her sexual history. Fortunately she'd had two glasses of wine before that session and was happy to comply.

"I got introduced to sex when I was seven, too, but it was just a kiss. I liked it, but the teacher caught us and sent us to detention. So I associated the pleasure part with guilt and shame. My parents weren't comfortable talking to me about sex. Most of what I knew about it I got out of *Where Did I Come From?* That was the book my mother gave me when I was seven, so she wouldn't have to discuss the birds and the bees."

Hilly's instinct for puritanical shame was dispelled at a seventh-grade party after she and a classmate emerged from a closet looking disheveled.

"I acquired a reputation for being daring and racy," she said. "People started treating me with deference and respect. I liked that. It was my first taste of feeling worldly, sophisticated, and a little superior." After that, she developed her own split personality—straight-arrow, straight-A student and randy, nubile party girl. Sneaking out of the house after her 11:00 p.m. curfew, she turned into a joyriding sinner, swigging peppermint schnapps, shouting Violent Femmes lyrics, and getting to know the mysteries of young male bodies. One evening, without knowing what to call it, she engaged in oral sex with a guy who was still carrying a skateboard.

I learned more about Hilly's former sex life in that brief account than I'd been able to pry out of her in the years we'd been together. It provoked my curiosity—and a little discomfort. One night when we were sprawled naked on our bed, steam rising from the mattress, a wailing of cats outside aroused by our love cries, I asked her to tell me more. When she told me about Buford the pizza delivery boy and Tripp the hippie who'd made her knees weak and British Mick (the tattooed bartender who liked to get spanked) and Greek Nick and Norwegian Jaan—I began to suspect that she'd had more experience than she'd let on and felt a pang of insecurity. I wondered what she was really up to when she was "staying late at work" or "going to the gym."

"Where is this Tripp now?" I demanded to know. She laughed out loud.

Now that our backgrounds had been put on display, Dr.

Selman asked what sexual issues between us needed to be addressed.

"The second night we met, I told her about my two flaws," I said. "One, I screw up good relationships. When things are going well, my sexual confidence goes up and I end up straying. Second, I find it hard to resist any girl who comes after me, not that that happens too frequently, maybe a few times a year. But, I have a hard time saying no."

"One of my problems is paranoia and jealousy," Hilly said. "When he goes out late and I stay home, I have visions of betrayal."

"Why do you go out so late?" Dr. Selman asked.

"Some of it is the nightlife reporting I do," I said. "There's a chance I might go out tonight. There's a really good party for the *Aristocrats* movie."

"And he goes out by himself without you?" Dr. Selman said, turning as usual to Hilly.

"It depends. I started a new job that I love more than any other I've ever had. I used to go out more in the middle of the week, but now I'm afraid that if I don't get to bed by eleven o'clock, I won't perform on the job as well the next day. So I can't enjoy the nightlife as much, which is a shame. What happens is he goes out and I try to tell myself that this is fine, it's good that we can go our separate ways from time to time, and that we don't feel as if we're smothering each other. But sometimes I feel a little threatened. I know what it's like out there and I imagine all these gorgeous girls throwing themselves at him. . . ."

"Is it true?" said Dr. Selman. "Are all these girls throwing themselves at you?" I thought I could detect a spark of jealousy on his part, although Hilly's picture of me fighting off gorgeous girls was, in fact, the work of an overheated imagination. I let Dr. Selman writhe and stuck to the historical truth.

"After my experience with Tammy, I probably thought I was destined to have a hyperactive sex life." But my post-Tammy history was all failures and embarrassments. "One day in the third grade I tried to bribe a girl named Shannon to say 'I love you' with four or five silver dollars. That's weird, right? She said it but didn't really mean it, so I threw the coins on the ground and walked away. That's disturbing, right?"

"George, that's cruel. We've got to find that poor girl so you can make amends with her!" Hilly was visibly worried.

Fear of rejection drove me to comic books, my beer-can collection, sports, and other manly pursuits. My preadolescent "sex life" was confined to an album in my mother's closet of maternal-looking nudes, a picture of Farrah Fawcett, that sort of thing.

"Then in the sixth grade Victoria dumped me—her last name began with a *D*—when someone wrote GG HAS VD on the playground wall."

"How is this relevant to your relationship now?" Dr. Selman asked.

"Well, if I'd had a normal, Hilly-type girl when I was young, maybe I wouldn't have gotten so screwed up."

In high school I stared for hours at photos of girls in the school's facebook. There wasn't any opportunity to socialize with them. Down the mountain they'd come in buses for class, then back up the mountain they'd go. "No wonder I have difficulty relating to reality?" I said.

I couldn't get Dr. Selman to bite. "This is like digging in a mine and no one's going to hit gold," he said. Whenever I'd try to bring up an experience that might relate to my sexual identity, he'd question its relevance and sometimes get on my case: "Why are you saying this in front of Hilly?" But talking about this stuff in front of Hilly was just the point. I wanted her to know where I'd come from, to understand and react. I thought it might help us unravel some of the issues that troubled our relationship. Our sex life was important to our future as a couple and to our understanding of ourselves. Wasn't unraveling these knots what therapy was supposed to be all about?

"Another thing: maybe if I hadn't been locked up in boarding school, I'd have developed into a normal human being," I said when the conversation was lagging. Dr. Selman allowed me to elaborate.

"It was like being in a penitentiary," I said. "The girls' school was five miles up Skiff Mountain. If you got caught up there after lights-out, you'd be rewarded with a twenty-hour work project for being AWOL. To be discovered in a room with a member of the opposite sex could have resulted in expulsion."

We were exiles in a wasteland of desire. Deprivation created a cult of onanism. There was no official rule against self-abuse at Kent. However, if you were ever caught "spanking" or "snapping," it was social suicide. When you walked into class, your classmates would snap their fingers in unison. A plump, rosy-cheeked boy who was allegedly busted, meat in hand, became known as the Red Snapper. A kindhearted, rail-thin geek nicknamed Rambo Tambo was ruined when someone discovered a portable false vagina (a "pocket pussy") under his mattress. (After that he became known as Hot Pocket.)

Thanks to the honor system, students couldn't lock the door of their rooms for a little privacy. Some renovated rooms had a lower drawer in the closet that, if pulled out, could effectively prevent someone from barging in, thereby giving the dolphin waxer a few extra seconds to lose his wood, but even that was dicey. "I caught you! You were spanking it!" I once heard a hard-core stoner screaming as he ran up and down the North Dorm hallway like Paul Revere. "Oh, yes, you were! Hey, everybody, I caught Rand rubbing one out! Busted!"

One classmate, utterly unashamed of his natural urges, was dubbed Le Roi du Spanque. Every semester Jean-Paul always made sure to claim the bottom bunk, where he would build himself a little tent, a shrine for the "heinous crime." He also kept hard-core porn mags with Danish captions in his foot-locker.

When pipes were about to burst, most Kentians hit a bath-room stall, but danger lurked even there. One could easily be discovered by classmates on the lookout for flailing feet under-neath the doors or by more aggressive narcs randomly peek-ing over them. Another strategy was to whip up a batch in the science building bathroom. If it was locked for the night, you might have to paddle a canoe down the Housatonic, hike up the Appalachian Trail, or build a spank shack atop Mount Algo.

"The other feature of life at Kent that I think permanently scarred me was the torment I suffered at the hands of the school's jocks," I said. "These sadistic barbarians hazed me and my fellow weaklings unmercifully, they punched us whenever the mood struck them, slapped us with hockey sticks, forced some of us to compete in cracker races—you had to run up a flight of stairs with a cracker in the cheeks of your butt, and if you dropped it, you had to eat it—paraded around the dorm naked, snapping their towels at us. And the school treated them as heroes to be looked up to."

"So there was some underlying homosexuality?" said Dr. Selman. It seemed as if he'd missed the brutality aspect of my recitation. He was right about the true (latent perhaps) nature of the jocks in my opinion, but I took his comment as a sly implication about my own sexual orientation.

"I am very conservative sexually," I protested. "I have never, ever done anything other than having some slightly irregular daydreams."

I did manage to lose my virginity three weeks before high school graduation. In college, I always found a way to sabotage budding romances, whether out of fear of rejection or fear of commitment. One girl, who proclaimed on our first date that she was going to marry me, got so tired of my love letters and phone calls that she ended up threatening to call the police if I ever showed up at her doorstep again. After that, I vowed to avoid involvement with anyone I might get emotionally attached to. I sought out misfits with whom there was no potential for a lasting or wholesome relationship.

"Can I just tell you about Clementine?" I said. "And then I'll be finished." Dr. Selman looked into his hands as if he were hoping to find a weapon he could use to silence me.

I met Clementine in French lit class. She was a tiny, fetching Gallic girl who in the sea of prim sorority girls stood out like a starving beast. She had a beguiling yet deranged look. Her eyes darted around as if enemies menaced her. She was always muttering curses or magic spells. The moment I saw her, I was bewitched. I figured that if I wasn't going to make it in the conventional college arena, I'd go over to the dark side. Also, I thought I had a better chance with a girl who seemed psychotic.

Clementine would come over to my pad, talk gibberish to herself, dance around, do the cancan, then put her hands to her mouth. "Oh, my Georgie, I'm starving, I'm soofering. Can you spare anything? May I take those pennies for a Creamy

Club at the Yello Sub? Oh, thank you, my Georgie. When I come back, I'll put on those glasses and stoody your coq! And then we have a fuck-fuck."

One night in the bar across the street, Clementine caught me talking to another girl. Clementine attacked me, flailing her arms, spitting in my face, and threatening to take off all her clothes and call the police. For some reason, the worse she behaved, the more I was attracted to her. I invited her to meet the folks that summer. On my mother's advice, I took her to see a psychiatrist. Clementine made a scene in his office. She told a dirty joke about a well-hung Pakistani guy "curing" a neurotic Frenchwoman. At a house party in Westport, Connecticut, she threatened to call the police on everyone, then hid under a bed. She walked around in circles in the backyard, talking and chain-smoking. Then she sat on the living room couch in her wet bathing suit and kept asking, "Where's Georgie, where's Georgie, have you seen my Georgie?" Then one day, out of the blue, she asked me to marry her.

"Marriage!" That did it. She'd just uttered the dreaded word. The commitment-free illusion was shattered. The exotic, bohemian vixen turned out to be a Betty Crocker homemaker in search of a docile mate. When I demurred, she unleashed a storm of abuse. I felt the noose tighten. I gave her a hasty good-bye and ran. I never saw Clementine again.

Harping on my sexual escapades backfired in more than one way. Instead of arousing Hilly's empathy and understanding, my tales of past adventures aroused more jealousy and mistrust. When Dr. Selman asked her for a reaction, she didn't rhapsodize about how "cute" my stories were. She focused on my real and imagined infidelities.

"He cheated on me once," she said. "I forgave him. That once. I can't predict what would happen if he did it again. He still flirts a lot."

"So why should she trust you now?" asked Dr. Selman. I tried to defend myself. I begged for slack. But the two of them ganged up on me, or so it seemed.

I blamed my flirtations and infidelities on Tammy: "She derailed my childhood." I repeated my formula: if I'd met Hilly sooner, I might have turned out okay. "Maybe I wouldn't still get into those horny trances or flirt with girls at two a.m." I wanted Dr. Selman to give me a clinical analysis that would give me some kind of formal model I could try to work my way out of.

"How can I change if I don't know what's the matter with me?" I said. Neurotic, obsessive-compulsive, infantile-arrested, stuporous melancholia, hebephrenic schizophrenia, barythymia, poikilothymia. I'd settle for anything as long as it was concrete.

"I need a verdict," I said.

"Don't be so dramatic," said Hilly.

"I just want to be taken seriously," I said.

"Are you sure you're not trying to get a laugh?" said Dr. Selman. On cue, I tried to take us back to the mirror and my fantasy world.

"Could I tell him about how we had sex watching *Children of the Damned*?" I said. Hilly gave me the nod, but I could see her cringe. "Sometimes I ask her to speak in an Austrian or Asian accent when we're having sex. Once or twice I asked her to wear pigtails and animal-head slippers or kneesocks and to pretend to be deaf, dumb, and blind."

"You realize he's not being serious now, don't you?"

"Well, I did once ask Hilly to put on a red wig, go out in the hallway for five minutes, then knock on the door as if she'd gotten the wrong room, something I got from a Fellini movie."

"That made me think you wanted to imagine you were having sex with someone else," Hilly said.

"That's the point. Doesn't that show a divided self, an inability to be grounded in reality? Sometimes I like to do it on the couch with the blinds up."

Dr. Selman finally delivered the clinical analysis I'd sought, pronouncing the same judgment he had when I told him about my grade-school escapades: "That sounds exhibitionistic."

"Wow! I feel like I'm back in Mr. Jones's class and you're about to send me home again for my antisocial behavior. I'm falling into one of my trances now. Tammy? Hilly? Tammy-Hilly. Will one of you please come to my rescue and liberate me from the prison of my woes?"

Finally Hilly and Dr. Selman laughed.

"Well, where do we go from here?" I asked Dr. Selman as the session drew to a close.

"Where do you go?" he said. "I suggest you go home and have sex."

CHAPTER TEN

INGA'S ACADEMY: HOW INGA TAUGHT HILLY HOW TO ENSNARE GEORGE

Hilly began one session by saying she developed a Jekyll and Hyde personality in her early twenties: "I was a competent overachiever and cruiser of the lower depths, not unlike Diane Keaton's character in *Looking for Mr. Goodbar*, my favorite movie at the time. She was a nice schoolteacher by day and sexual deviant at night."

"Isn't she murdered at the end?" Dr. Selman asked. "What was going on with you back then?"

"I was so torn between my feelings of disgrace and my sexual longing that I developed an alter ego. During the day I was poised, efficient, and reliable—my boss adored me and trusted me with everything. But as soon as I left the office, I'd race downtown, change into a much racier outfit, throw down a martini or two, hop into a cab, and head to 7B, the East Village bar where my friend Sharon Tate and I would stay out all night, teasing and flirting with all kinds of bad boys."

"Sharon Tate, as in the actress murdered by the Manson family?" Dr. Selman asked.

"That was her nickname. She was a look-alike, which really helped with the boys. I became known at 7B as Hilary Distillery. I was really into martinis. We had a ball, but eventually I developed a chip on my shoulder regarding men. I took great pleasure in luring guys to my apartment and then abusing them with vivid putdowns, sometimes pretending to have forgotten their names, mocking their attempts to perform sexually, and humiliating them as much as I could. And it didn't help that my mother was constantly chiding me for being single. She actually encouraged me to spend my vacations on singles cruises instead of going home. When I turned twenty-five, she sent me a photograph of herself and my father inside my birthday card, and on the back of it she wrote, 'Me and your father at age 25, when I had just become engaged.'"

"Hilly, why was it so hard for you to believe that someone would want a relationship with you?" Dr. Selman asked.

"Because I still felt like a fat, thirteen-year-old girl daydreaming about Duran Duran, and on top of that I never dealt with my associations of sex with guilt and shame, so I couldn't fathom any guy wasting his time with someone like me."

"Hilly used to practice witchcraft," I said. "She cast a few spells on guys before me when she was having trouble landing a boyfriend."

Dr. Selman seemed intrigued, but noticed that Hilly was staring at the floor. "Is this something you'd rather not discuss?" he asked her.

"Why—are you scared?" she said, suddenly giddy. "It was only *one* spell, and it was because I lived near Morgana's Chamber, a little store on West Tenth Street that specialized in the dark arts. Around that time I met Chad at the lesbian barbecue place across from my apartment. We were both sitting at the bar eating Frito pie and just started talking. He'd seen me there several times and thought it was cute how I liked Frito pie so much. Chad was so handsome, so nice, and we had sooo much in common. Music, movies, food, plus he only lived two blocks from me—it seemed too good to be true! Over the next few months, we really got to know each other, e-mailing every day, talking on the phone for *hours*. I was able to find out that he'd struck it superrich during the dot-com boom and was twenty-nine. Now he was basically semiretired, and trying to figure out what to do next; he couldn't decide between becoming a deejay and sailing around the world. Oh, and I think his family had money, too. Anyway, we started dating, and Chad seemed to be taking the relationship at a pace that I appreciated. Didn't seem to be in any kind of rush. Unlike every other jerk who'd hit the jackpot in the late nineties, he was humble, soft-spoken, laid-back, polite, with a self-deprecating sense of humor, and drank moderately. He was so masculine and athletic! And did I mention drop-dead gorgeous? After two months of holding hands, making out, and having so much fun, I was kind of ready to take things to the next level, you know. So I went inside Morgana's Chamber and bought a few books and other supplies so I could help move things along. The spell I cast was meant to attract love. It involved candles and a small voodoo doll representing Chad that I had to anoint with oil, place in a wooden box, and then bury in my backyard after midnight during a full moon. The following evening he took me to a romantic dinner at One if by Land, Two if by Sea. There was a lot of meaningful eye contact, and we even talked about going surfing together in Costa Rica, fantasizing about starting a beach bar in Hawaii. Afterward I managed to lure him back to his apartment—the spell was working! Everything was going great—we were making out furiously in the elevator, attacking each other in the hallway . . . and then we entered his enormous penthouse apartment. Oh my God, it was a duplex. There were so many *rooms*; the guy had, like, six bathrooms, and there was an entire room for his elaborate sound system. It was like a little discotheque in there. He had *thousands* of albums arranged in alphabetical order and first put on a Nina Simone record, which was the perfect choice and totally gave me goose bumps! The entire place was immaculate—he had to have had a maid who came every day. Oh! And there was this beautiful spiral staircase that led to the roof, which was all *his*! He said something about wanting to put a pool up there. So far, this was becoming the best night of my life. It was January, and he had a fire roaring in his fireplace, and we're passionately writhing around on his Maison Jansen sofa, both of us half-naked, heavy petting getting heavier, and my head is about to explode! It couldn't have been any better than this, so I said, 'Let's just get completely naked. I'll do anything you want.' With that, he stopped, stood up, and walked to the other end of the apartment, which was like fifty yards away. I assumed he was getting a condom, but five, ten minutes passed. I was beginning to get paranoid, like he was a Patrick Bateman type and he was looking for his chain saw. He came back fully dressed.

"'What's wrong? What happened? What did I do?' I said, practically in tears. He didn't say anything for about thirty seconds. He just went over to his stereo room and started polishing the records, putting them in their sleeves, and turning off all the power buttons. 'Should I go?' I asked him.

"'Maybe so. It's getting kind of late,' he softly replied. He said he was sorry and offered to walk me home, but I just left."

Dr. Selman snapped out of his trance. "What the hell was wrong with this guy? What happened? Why?"

"Whatever it was, I never found out. I figured he had intimacy issues. I don't know, maybe he had a green weenie."

"No doubt brought on by your spell," Dr. Selman said. The three of us laughed in unison for the first time.

Hilly was in bad shape post-Chad. Fortunately her friend Inga helped her get over it. She was Hilly's best friend at the time and was the kind of girl who knew how to ensnare any man. She was found in a bush in Asia and adopted. She'd grown up all over Europe, went to a fancy boarding school, and now wanted to infiltrate high fashion and the world of hip-hop. Above all she wanted to find herself a nice gangsta boyfriend, and to achieve that dream she practiced Ebonics: "Hilly dawg, you look bootylicious for reals. Do the math, ho."

One night Hilly met Inga at the white-hot restaurant Moomba. They got into boyfriend issues and Hilly admitted she was having some problems. "Why can't I just date someone I like? What's wrong with me?" she asked Inga.

"Are you serious about this?" said Inga with a slight Swedish accent. "You fo' real? Because if you are, you must enroll in Inga's Academy. You have to do *exactly* what I say." Hilly agreed to sign up as Inga's student.

Rule 1: *"First, you must eat,"* said Inga. "So many girls don't eat or pretend to eat. This makes them appear high maintenance and irritating and shit? Guys like girls with a healthy appetite, especially red-meat eaters. So order a big steak, rare. Trust me, it's a real turn-on and I'm not straight trippin'." (A hard one: Hilly had been a vegetarian since high school.)

Rule 2: *"Having some pudge is key,"* Inga continued. "Skinny girls may be nice to look at, but guys actually think they're kind of gross. Aight? Pudge feels better to them even though we think it's disgusting. A real man wants some bangin' badonkadonk to grab. The main thing to remember is there are two things always on a guy's mind: *food and sex*. Always show up at his crib with food, never show up empty-handed."

Rule 3: "*Be fun and laid-back.* So keep taking your Prozac, Hills, and if you have a meltdown, stay home and get over it. Don't ever go his place frazzled, uptight, paranoid, or all nervous and shit. You gots to hold it down, sista." Inga suggested finding an inspirational role model, such as Bridget Fonda in *Jackie Brown*, who's supercool, totally comfortable, and unintimidated around guys, even sleazy ones packing heat.

Rule 4: "*Never be a burden, demanding, or a managerial fussbudget.* You want him to light up any time he thinks of you or hears your name. You want him to put you on the same level as his stupid guy friends, so he's not worried or apprehensive to call or see you. So don't do annoying things like ask him, 'Why didn't you call me last night?' Or, 'We *really* need to talk.' Never say, 'Are we still on for brunch tomorrow? Because my friends want to meet you. Oh, and make sure you wear your khakis and iron them this time, sweetie!' Boo that. Also don't ask to go to a specific restaurant or club or try to change a guy, mold him into an accessory to your lifestyle. It doesn't work that way. That being said, you and I know we both want to go to Moomba, it just can't look that way."

Rule 5: "*Never be overly optimistic.* Because men are all pretty much ignorant tools and fools, and they're always going to be that way, so don't expect too much. However, because they're dumb, you can attract them with—what?"

"I don't know, by having big boobs?" Hilly asked.

"*Wrong*. With food and sex. Again, those two things are always at the forefront of their minds, so keep them there. This is cake, girl. And cook for them." Hilly said she didn't know how. "Then find out what he likes and buy it at Balducci's."

Rule 6: "*Don't have sex right away.* There has to be a story, an interlude, some drama, and many stages," Inga said. "So don't give it up too fast. Keep denying the guy. Oral sex is fine if you really like the guy. Sex is different. The guy must know that even after that tease of a bj, he still has to work for the pot of gold."

Rule 7: *"Never deny a guy sex once you've fallen for him and con-summated the relationship.* Until you get married, never say no if the guy wants to have sex, even if you're in a terrible mood with PMS or feel fat, bloated, and disgusting. If you're having your period and it's not that bad, have sex with him anyway. Just do it, lay down, get it over with, because it'll be over in a few minutes. Ain't no thang. The only time you can say no is if you have one-hundred-percent proof he's been cheating."

Rule 8: *"Don't be needy,* don't be calling a guy too much, es-pecially when you're lonely or getting your Sancerre on late at night. Don't always pick up the phone when he calls or call him back right away. Be elusive. Keep the ball in your court, dawgy. Better to have all the power than be out of control, devastated, and crying. Aight?"

Rule 9: One day while Inga was looking around Hilly's apartment, she said "high technology" was important to guys, so Hilly needed a cordless phone and a DVD player. *"Always have three or four movies around* because, otherwise, what are you gonna do? You can't have *sex.* And they have to be the right kind—no *Basic Instinct,* no *9½ Weeks,* no psycho-chick stuff. They should be newish action thrillers with an edgy side, with a few racy sex scenes. Not too racy though, not soft porn. If there's a boob shot and then someone comes in and shoots the guy, that's fine. It all good."

Rule 10: *"Guys like beer, so always have some in the fridge.* Like four or five Heinekens and leave them there, don't drink them."

Rule 11: *"Guys like salty snacks, so get some Doritos.* You want him to feel like he's having fun, like he's at his buddy's house but it smells better and he's with a hot chick. Remember, guys are *really* dumb. Food and sex. One more thing."

Rule 12: *"Be comfortable naked.* Hilly, even though we know we're fat because we're in fashion, right, you have to remember that guys like pudge. Pudge is sex. Because it's soft and warm and guys like girls to be comfortable about it. So walk around naked like it's no big deal. Don't cover your boobs or butt when you get up to use the bathroom. Being embarrassed is not sexy."

Before Inga left, she inspected Hilly's wardrobe. "Parts of your outfits are good. But you're always wearing the latest fashionable thing—new shoes, matching bag, everything co-ordinated and top-of-the-line. That's all good for having lunch at Bergdorf's, but you don't want to look uptight and unap-proachable because then you'll end up living here alone."

Rule 13: *"Keep the hair always long, always down, remember your boobs, replace the tweed A-line skirt with a pair of jeans, and keep the high heels.* Ya heard?"

For Hilly's first assignment, Inga set her up with a photo assistant, Gunner. "Go get him, he's just a *loser*, a scrub! Pimp the system and holla back tonight!"

"Okay, hella cool," Hilly said. Gunner was a kickboxing in-structor on the side and, according to Hilly, an "Adonis." What the heck, she thought, I'll follow her advice and see what hap-pens. Lo and behold she immediately had Gunner in the palm of her hand. She experimented with a few more guinea pigs, and all of Inga's methods worked. If Hilly ever hit a snag, she'd think, what would Inga do now? That would work, too!

And then she met George.

CHAPTER ELEVEN

THE WORLD ACCORDING TO PTOLEMY

My friend Ptolemy, who's dedicated to keeping me on the path of corruption, offered an alternative book of etiquette for young males. Not *How to Get Your Girl* but *How to Avoid Getting Gotten* by her was his theme. The subtext was his anxiety that I might be drifting from the fraternal bond that had kept us acting like juvenile delinquents as we approached middle age.

Compared to Inga, Ptolemy was a more satanic kind of counselor. Like his namesake, Ptolemy thought that the world was the center of the universe. But like Steinberg's famous cartoon, he thought it was circumscribed by the boundaries of Manhattan, more specifically the small galaxy of Manhattan bars he frequented and generously subsidized.

I remember a cab drive across Bleecker Street, not long after he'd had a heart attack, when Ptolemy claimed he'd been a regular at every bar we passed—Kenny's Castaways . . . the Red Lion . . . the Back Fence . . . Milano's . . . and many more. His philosophy of life could be epitomized as Everything to Excess.

A burly 240-pounder now, he often appears in a three-piece suit, sporting a homburg, the burlesque version of a gentleman. An expert mimic, a legendary bon vivant, Ptolemy has worked as a carpenter, stockbroker, lifeguard, waiter, nightclub doorman, screenwriter, bit player in movies. He's sold vacuum cleaners, mushrooms, guns, owned a half-dozen bars, and lived in a homeless shelter.

At times I've thought he was a figment, a Mr. Potato Head amalgam of all my mischievous friends and Damien impulses that are locked in eternal battle with the earnest, straight-arrow, Cub Scout side of my personality. Ptolemy has been my best friend since adolescence. He and I used to shoot guinea-pig pellets through a straw at classmates' and teachers' heads. He was there when I smoked my first cigarette behind the Met and also the first time I got drunk, at my mother's wedding reception. He was there snickering behind me in detention (for "gross improper judgment" and "lying to medical staff" to get out of class). He was in the next room laughing like a hyena when my stepfather was reading me the riot act for wrecking his Jaguar and deflowering my younger brothers' Belgian nanny (on the same night).

He was always egging me on, whether the game was throwing snowballs at bus drivers or firing bottle rockets at cars. Ptolemy prescribed six shots of tequila to steady the nerves before any act of vandalism. He conducted our joint vomiting sessions like Toscanini conducting an orchestra. He's held my hand on numerous occasions when I've driven girlfriends out of my life. His favorite way to express approval or fondness is to spit a mouthful of beer on a colleague's blue blazer. Together we have hid behind hedges when prep school proctors with bloodhounds searched for the perpetrators of some whimsical crime. Together we have eluded the police on East Hampton low-speed chases.

Good-natured roughhousing has escalated into bona fide fisticuffs at times. One row began innocently with hurled birthday cakes and ended with bloody punches and kicks in the back of a cab. At the Gold Rush once, he became enraged by my suggestion that we move on to another bar and lifted me off the floor by the throat. Early one evening at Siberia, my monologue eulogizing Ayn Rand provoked him to begin slapping my head like a rubber ball. In response, I cast a tequila shot in his direction. Within seconds we were crashing into the jukebox and I was pinned face-first on the filthy floor. "Say *uncle*, say *uncle*!" he screamed.

Cock-blocking was another way we toyed with fraternal bonds. Later that night, I watched him hypnotizing a doe-eyed lass. My thoughts were on revenge. When he was distracted for a moment, I sped to her side and whispered some intelligence about one of Ptolemy's porny sexual fetishes, bukkake. It worked. She gave me a bug-eyed look and fled the bar. Once, when he had managed to maneuver a winsome maid into a bedroom at my mother's house, I persuaded my brother Austin to burst into the room with a camera and take a flash.

"I was about to get laid!" Ptolemy cried as the half-dressed girl made her escape. We had debates about whether a true friend should always act as a wingman or whether cock-blocking was morally justifiable, even noble. When he was the victim, Ptolemy became judgmental, condemning the sport as uncool, immoral, envious, tantamount to tripping a handicapped marathon runner. "You should really look into this, maybe ask Dr. Selman. I mean, you can't get laid because you have a girlfriend, so I shouldn't either? That's communism." When he was the agent, he defended cock-blocking as the intervention of a big brother to prevent his junior sibling from making a disastrous hookup. "That's like a benign dictatorship situation." When he came down from the pulpit, however, a mischievous smile crossed his face and he defended cock-blocking as a high form of comic entertainment. "That's hilarious—I will never forget this night!"

When Ptolemy first met Hilly, he expressed approval with a wolfish leer. A few weeks later, when he learned that she and I were still together, he ground his teeth and began counseling me.

"Try to maintain a rotation of at least *four* women in your life. If you don't do this, your manhood will wither away, and Hilly will be repelled. You think she'll be attracted to a clinger? The key is to have multiple liaisons on the sly. Remember, it's not cheating unless you remember her name."

Once Hilly and I had achieved the status of "an item," he warned me that she was "crazy." He even tried to make out with her in the back of a cab, and when that didn't work out, he stooped to cock-blocking in extremis.

"We caught him masturbating in boarding school," he told Hilly.

She just laughed. "So have I," she returned.

It was pretty clear that my drift in the direction of commitment threatened him.

One night we started off at Milano's bar on Houston Street. "Oh, man, I can't believe you got me out tonight," I moaned.

"Bullshit," he replied, staring me down. "Getting *you* to go out is so easy, it's like giving a retarded kid a lollipop." After feeding the jukebox a $5 bill and buying a round, Ptolemy warned me to watch out for hot girls such as Hilly. "Listen, don't get me wrong, I'm not saying Hilly's a waste of time, but most hot girls like her are. What you really need to do is find an ugly-hot chick. The French call it *jolie-laide*. You know, like a girl who's got a little something wrong with her. Maybe she got mistreated, she's missing a tooth, she's walking with a limp, a little wounded—something you can pinpoint so, you know, you can bring 'em down. That is, *if* you wanna get laid. Let me tell you about an Oscar party I went to: the *Gossip Girl* cast was there with all their hot friends—really good-looking, wearing expensive boots and designer jeans and fucking cashmere sweaters—really well pulled together. And I was like, there's a lot going on with that. Because even though they were really pretty, I knew it wasn't even worth saying hello. Dude, to even get a phone number you'd have to plan the most amazing elaborate night of your life, and then they probably still wouldn't bang you."

We moved on to Mars Bar down the street. The barmaid remembered Ptolemy from the Bellevue Bar. I was getting increasingly tipsy and turning into Captain Wasted, ordering beers, swigging from a flask, putting my arm around strange homeless-looking dudes, and dancing around—at one point up on the bar.

"Let me tell you about something I like to call the 'bang-to-work ratio,'" Ptolemy said, after sitting me down. "Truth is, if it's too much work, it's not worth it. You have to be honest with yourself: Do I want to be obligated to keep calling and hanging out with this girl? Or have I really kind of done what I need to do, and can I move on and find someone new and less annoying? Here's an example: I was expecting to enjoy this one girl recently. She took her clothes off, hot little brunette, curvy, genuinely nice boobs, pretty cool, a photographer or something, and then it was 'Blah blah blah blah blah,' this Muppet babbling all the time. So I asked, 'Are you fucking talking right now? Shut up!' and she started crying! It sucked. After five bangs I had to let her go. People were like, 'You broke up with that chick?! She's totally hot! You're lucky she went out with you.' And I had to explain, 'Yeah, man, I guess you're right, but you don't understand what it was *like.* It was unsexy, painful—there was a lot going on inside that crazy head.' She wasn't worth more than a few bangs. Five was way too many.

"Don't let me confuse you—it's *okay* to re-bang under certain circumstances. If I've planted the flag, I might do it again, maybe one more time. I try to average banging each girl 4.7 times, *max.* If she's willing to let you call her up in the middle of the night when you're drunk and come over, that's a good sign. If she's going to make herself available to you *anytime,* that's a keeper. She might even make it into the teens, bangs-wise. But in general, if it's something where you have to take her to dinner, introduce her to your friends, or endure her presence in the harsh glare of sobriety, then only one to three bangs.

"That being said, if she's a total knockout, you don't want to cast her away after three bangs; you'll want to milk that for a while, even if she's really annoying. Crazy's a whole nother thing. Either way, what you want to do is burn her into your consciousness, into the spank bank, for those times you have nothing to bang, you need to whack it, and there's no Russian porn around for some reason."

Next stop, Tom & Jerry's on Elizabeth Street. We both knew a few people there. I discussed marriage with a young Midwestern woman I'd just met. It was her idea to elope. By now things had degenerated into an epic rager, but Ptol was still holding forth articulately.

"I'm happy to have sex with hot girls," he said, smoking outside. "And, listen, I *appreciate* them having sex with me. Who isn't overjoyed at the prospect of getting laid? But remember a few things: First of all, the *first* bang is always the sweetest. Period. Secondly, inevitably you're going to discover that she's not as hot as you thought she was or she's incredibly irritating, boring, or has nothing to say. Most chicks are like that. I mean, I was banging this girl Madison, who, incidentally, reminds me of Hilly, physically. She had an incredible body, the head and the body were a solid match, her boobs were almost *Playboy*-caliber boobs—they looked fake but they *weren't*. Normally I see a hot chick and think something like, if only she had Malin Akerman's head on Jessica Alba's body, but I didn't think that with Madison. She was Southern, like twenty-three, very sexy, and great. But I'm pretty sure she was mildly retarded because I couldn't understand what she was saying half the time. It was like she had a mouthful of buffalo balls. Anyway, I went through the wooing motions—took her out a couple times, really charmed her, you know, put in the *time*. Finally I boned her and it was great! A couple more times and it was awesome. But then, after a while, it became depressing, and even though she was so hot, the thought of spending any time with her depressed the shit out of me. I was, like, I'd rather just masturbate, man. I couldn't talk to her on the phone because her accent was so thick, and, regardless, she only wanted to talk about tanning, *Project Runway*, and *The Bachelor*. Listen to me—I really *wanted* her to be smart, engaging, cool, and I tried my best to give her a chance because she was a hot chick, so I went the extra mile. I was like, 'How can *I* help *you*?' But there was only so much I could do. I regrettably had to just kind of phase her out. The bang-to-work/torture ratio was just too disproportionate. Watch out for that, man, I know what it's like."

Back inside, Ptolemy ran into what he would later describe as a "somewhat attractive" chick "with helmet problems" (translation: "a butter face") whom he knew. They went into the bathroom, made out, and fondled each other's privates. "I actually pulled my cock out but she would only touch it," he confided minutes later. "Definitely will be banging that soon, I think. Whatever. She's already in the spank bank."

Walking east on Houston Street, I finally convinced Ptolemy that Hilly was the first girl I thought I had a chance of a real relationship with, and that she was the first girl I felt really cared about me. He acquiesced with a few bits of sage advice. "I'm sorry to hear you say that. Nevertheless, there's one last piece of advice I can offer you, Gurley: You *must* start banging another girl at once. You want to maintain a healthy relationship with Hilly? Remember that it is in man's *nature* to cheat. Cheating can be a way of finding out whether your number one relationship is valid. It's a good thing to jolt you out of your comfort zone. Also, science has proven that without an illicit affair every three months a man starts to become effeminate. Speaking of which, why are you wearing UGG boots?"

"My mom got me them for Christmas. I don't care, they're comfy."

"And extremely gay. As I was saying, keep in mind that it's not technically cheating if you get sucked off as long as Hilly doesn't find out. If *you* don't feel guilty, you're *not* guilty. Anything that feels good cannot be morally wrong. Infidelity is infidelity of the heart, the soul, and the spirit. You can share your body promiscuously as long as you do not share your heart."

We were pretty drunk by this point. Yet Ptolemy was still able to deliver some words of wisdom that encapsulated his code when it came to the fair sex.

"It's also not cheating if you're outside the territorial boundaries of the United States," he said at Mekong on King Street. "So leave town a lot without telling her and see how she reacts. Another one to remember: Having sex with someone who can advance your *career* isn't cheating. You should also buy Hilly a copy of *Deviant Desires* and see if you can get her to play along with Pony Play or Balloon Fetishes. If she winces, it's a sign that she won't be open-minded to trying new things.

"Which brings to mind a few extenuating circumstances that may come your way: If a girl is doing research on a sex toy and asks for your help, go for it. Anything to advance science. Or, if a really hot girl comes to you and says she's worried that she might be a lesbian and wants to have sex with you to find out, have a little compassion and *oblige*. It would be cruel and insensitive for Hilly to ever complain.

"Now turn on your tape recorder," he said. "It's on? Good. This one's the ace in the hole, top secret stuff. Don't tell anyone. I don't want this getting around. This never fails. Here's what you do. You go into a bar, only you don't go in empty-handed. You're working on something. You're working on a book, a magazine article, whatever. You sit down, order a drink, and don't say anything. You start scribbling in your notebook. You're the only guy in the bar not checking out the female bartender. Don't ever call them barmaids. They hate that. You're working, nose to the grindstone. And at some point, inevitably, she's going to come over to ask you a question: 'What are you working on?' And you're going to say, 'I'm working on a book. . . . I'm writing a book on *relationships*. I've been interviewing a lot of married guys.' Right away, you've got her hooked. You're writing a book about guys that like watching *Project Runway* or the Bravo channel, whatever, something gay, metrosexual, but interesting to women. Has to be what women are into and has to have some dull edges.

"I can't *believe* I'm giving this away. You don't deserve it. All right. What you want is the *girl*, this smoking-hot barmaid who will blow you if you play your cards right. So you ask her to give you some suggestions for your make-believe book. You have to take her very seriously, though. This isn't some parlor game. This is a foolproof, fireproof, guaranteed method to getting laid. But you have to be professional, not weird or goofy as is your wont. After she gives you a tidbit about guys or relationships, then you blow her off. You say, 'Okay, thanks. Hey, someone over there wants a drink,' and you don't smile, you don't wink, nothing. You start taking notes again. And she stands behind the bar looking at you, her imagination is on fire. 'This mysterious guy is somehow different, I've got to have him.' At five a.m., you're still there, still scribbling, the last customer. You offer to help her clean up, you tell her she saved your life with her insights, and you notice she's looking at you with these feline, jungle eyes, and the deal is closed, slam dunk, works every time. You won't have to make a move or say a single witty thing. Your place or hers, that's the only thing left to decide.

"And it's always best to do your banging at her place, by the way. If that's impossible, then make sure you clean up after, because bimbos always leave something behind as evidence— an earring, a pubic hair, some panties, a thank-you note. Some kind of chick-territorial thing. Let's see, here are a few more miscellaneous rules off the top of my head, if you *really* like Hilly," Ptolemy continued. "Make her feel sorry for you. Dwell on your emotionally complicated childhood. Tell her you find sex more than once a month abhorrent.

"Oh, I mention that already? What? And for God's sake don't ever let me hear you talk about marriage. Marriage equals death. Pal, I'm trying to save you. So whatsay we head for a nightclub!" Ptolemy cried out. We decided on Marquee for our last stop. At 3:00 a.m. Ptolemy and I were the only people upstairs, dancing basically together in our heavy winter coats and weirding people out. One of the managers began sending status updates to Facebook about our impromptu "dance-off." A mutual friend commented, "Team Gurley!" But a big African-American bouncer started following Ptol and me around, probably fearing that we would knock over someone's bottle or maybe start sucking each other off. We lost track of each other. When I headed to the bar, the bouncer saw me stumble, said I was "acting strange," and escorted me in the direction of the front door.

I looked back and saw my pal chatting up a girl half his age. Ptolemy, my Falstaff, I thought. We have heard the chimes at midnight. But if I am to save myself, I must send you back to Eastcheap alone.

CHAPTER TWELVE

SELMAN AGONISTES

"We've hit a wall," I said to Dr. Selman.

"We're not sure of where we're headed," Hilly chimed in.

"Sometimes we feel as if you're not cheering for the home team," I said. Our opening gambit was an ambush we'd been planning for several weeks. Although we'd had some laughs and good conversation in the early sessions, the dynamic between Dr. Selman and us remained tense. Hilly was uneasy about opening up. I was often disruptive. I couldn't get him to show an interest in my childhood. Hilly couldn't get him to interpret her dreams. When she told him about the dinosaurs that chase her up a spiral staircase, he looked at his watch as if to signal his lack of interest.

"I think the dinosaurs represent the tyrants I deal with in the fashion business—or maybe my landlord," she said.

"I suppose that interpretation is as good as any" was Dr. Selman's cool response. He seemed abstracted and guarded at the same time. He may have been daunted by the challenges we presented. So we decided to confront him again. After we'd spent a few minutes in a typical nondirectional ramble, I announced that we had some issues, some questions.

"Is that okay?" I said.

Dr. Selman gave a little shrug and raised an eyebrow. "I'm listening," he said with a profound lack of enthusiasm.

Hilly opened her bag and produced a crumpled sheet, which she unfolded and smoothed out. "'We're wondering why you don't ask us more personal questions,'" she read. "'You don't seem that curious about who we really are.' I don't understand why you don't want to know more about our formative years."

I was already regretting the overture and began to buckle. "Don't worry. The sessions we've had have been amazing. We've already learned so much. We're very grateful. It's just that after the last few, we've been confused. I was beginning to think I irritated you."

Dr. Selman regarded me in silence.

Hilly went on and I cringed some more. "'Sometimes we feel as if you're too critical of us and aren't interested in the positive aspects of our relationship.'"

I broke in again. "Sometimes you seem to be trying to pit us against each other. This will probably sound ridiculous and paranoid, but at times I've felt that you were trying to wake Hilly up to the fact that I'm a villain, that she's the innocent victim, and that she's crazy to put up with me."

Dr. Selman looked magnificently composed and said, "Keep going."

She read on, "'Sometimes you seem annoyed and angry, like you'd rather be getting a root canal. Other times you're warm and engaging. You laugh at us and with us. We don't know where we stand. We'd like to know what your opinion of us is in clear, precise language, and to stop saying things like "What does it matter what I think?"'"

My feet were getting colder, so I attempted to pander to him. "I know we've been hard to deal with. You're probably irked that we haven't taken your advice to read the codependency book."

No sign of approval or compassion. Dr. Selman's eyes might as well have been a pair of agates.

My voice seemed to have risen an octave and had acquired an unmistakable vibrato. "Maybe you're right—those are things to bring up in individual therapy? By the way, would it be off base to ask you for a sketch of your philosophy? Listen, this has been great for us, it really has. We're indebted to you. We don't want to second-guess you. We're absolutely certain you know what you're doing. But we need you to toss us a life buoy, give us a little progress report. We're committed to working things out, but we don't want to leave the sessions feeling worse. Something you said last time was a real bummer."

"What was that?" said Dr. Selman.

"When you said our relationship worked 'such as it is.' What does that mean, 'such as it is'?" Hilly put the piece of paper back in her bag and we waited in silence.

Dr. Selman smiled and cleared his throat. After six months of blank stares and scratching his chin, he delivered a provisional verdict.

"You have a good relationship in some sense. By that I mean that you've been together for a fairly long time. Despite everything, you're still together. If it was as bad as you sometimes make it out to be, you'd have split up long ago. So, somehow, it works. The question is, what will happen if you actually make a change?"

From the beginning, Dr. Selman had stressed the importance of keeping our eye on a goal and what we hoped to achieve. During the fourth session, Hilly said she'd love it if I were less controlling and irritable and able to make plans. I wanted to improve our relationship, make it "healthier" and to "break the routine," spice things up, try new things, not sit around watching TV and going to the same restaurants. I wanted us to find out more about each other before we made one step further. At the same time, I wanted to maintain the status quo.

"You've succeeded in that," Dr. Selman said. His tone suggested that was not a triumph. After all, it meant that we hadn't changed anything.

"That's not exactly a goal, is it?" I said. He wouldn't embellish. I guessed that he wanted us to figure things out on our own. It wasn't his job to be a cheerleader and tell us how great he thought we were. He was still unclear about Hilly's goals, but thought that we'd grown closer, "to some extent."

There's always a qualification, I thought. Never a seal of approval. Much later, I figured out that the stamp of approval had to come from us. A good relationship doesn't depend on a blue ribbon bestowed by someone else. But I hadn't reached that level of enlightenment.

"Can I say that sometimes you come across as a little sarcastic?" I said.

"You just said it."

"See—that sounded sarcastic." He actually laughed at that. I admitted that I sometimes tried to lead the sessions astray by throwing in riffs on my junior high basketball career or rants about joggers in the park. "But when I do that, do you have to respond with a 'Fascinating' dripping with sarcasm?"

"Maybe you're hearing something that's not really there." He added a solemn denial of any secret desire to turn Hilly against me.

"Maybe so, but that's how it sometimes feels," I said. "Doesn't the theory book say that we're entitled to our feelings?" Got him now, I thought. Checkmate.

"Maybe it's how you've begun to perceive yourself," Hilly chimed in. Ouch.

"It's called projection," Dr. Selman said. "You project onto me what you think yourself." I must have looked hurt, pathetic, because he gave me a pitying look. "Therapy is not fun. It can be painful." He repeated his comment that our relationship was "good" because we'd been together more than four years. Not perfect, but not without positives. It was what it was.

Hilly said she was sorry if we'd hurt his feelings. He made a gesture of shooing away a fly. It was all right, he said. He wore an imperious look that suggested, do you two little bugs think you have the power to hurt me?

"Are you sure you don't favor Hilly?" I persisted. "Don't you like her a little more than me?"

Now he gave me a grin. "She is better looking."

CHAPTER THIRTEEN

WAXING WROTH

"I call him Furious George or Mr. Grumpy when he gets into one of his moods," said Hilly. "A lot of things seem to make him nervous, anxious, cranky, sad, depressed—and angry."

"But not all those things at once," I said, groping for a little slack.

Hilly didn't hear. "If the remote goes missing in the couch, it's my fault for tidying up too much. He complains when I talk too much. He complains when I don't talk enough. He complains when I talk about things that are 'too mundane,' like jewelry and fashion. In other words, anything having to do with my job. He says, 'Please, I can't deal with this now . . . too materialistic . . . it's bringing me down . . . back to reality . . . talk about something else . . . anything.' When I talk too loudly, he blows up. 'I'm right here, you don't have to scream!' And he's screaming, telling me not to scream."

If she'd been saying that sort of thing to me, it would have led to an argument, maybe another shouting match. But, once again, because she was making these revelations to Dr. Selman, I was able to listen with a weird sense of detachment. I listened—and was appalled. Dr. Selman must have been thinking that I was not just an SOB and a scoundrel, but a smoldering powder keg, an unstable monster who belonged in a padded cell.

Tasting blood, I piled on and joined the George-bashing as if demonizing myself were fun. "She's right. If she doesn't give me enough attention or doesn't say the right thing, I blow up. I pick fights, make her cry, and then make fun of her crying. 'Oh, boo-hoo, I'm crying! I'm crying!' Pipe down and get over it! I blame her for my foul moods, my frustrations, my career downturn, whatever. Then I get scared of driving her away and apologize, promise never to do it again. But I keep pushing my luck and she keeps letting me get away with it."

"I gave him a Mr. Grumpy T-shirt as a stocking stuffer. He hates Christmas and all holidays except Easter."

"Hilly starts talking about Christmas around May," I said. "It's a sore subject. And not the only one. Sometimes she provokes me. I'm not letting myself off the hook, but I've told her a thousand times not to touch my belly button or my pinkie toes. She can't help herself."

"I understand his moodiness much better from having read *The Irritable Male Syndrome*," she told Dr. Selman. "It says that males experience different levels of testosterone, which can make them irritable, aggressive, or withdrawn at the drop of a hat. They can't explain it, it's not their fault, it's a chemical imbalance. Sometimes they feel 'emotionally sunburned.' Sometimes when I try to comfort him, I touch one of those sunburned spots and I end up making him feel worse. It's like a male version of PMS. One of my goals is to help minimize the outbursts."

Some of my complaints were borderline legitimate, such as

when Hilly stopped taking the Pill and failed to tell me for six weeks, though that didn't seem to faze Dr. Selman. He applauded her rationale: Hilly had "unconsciously" gone off birth control because she was overloaded with responsibilities. He congratulated her for being so open, honest, and insightful. At the time, I was flabbergasted. In retrospect, maybe it was justice because more often than not my peeves were either petty or insane.

Dr. Selman listened with apparent concern and, I thought, his usual bias in favor of Hilly, but how could it have been otherwise? And as usual, anytime I tried to deflect the topic, he'd blow the whistle.

"Let me see if I got this straight," he said. "Maybe I can rephrase it. What you're saying is that in addition to being critical and controlling, George is edgy, cross, huffy, easily annoyed, turbulent, mad, and irritable at times. Correct?" After a while it dawned on me that he wasn't picking on me so much as focusing on the obvious. "Why do you put up with all that, Hilly?" was a constant refrain. She tried to rationalize her attachment to me by explaining the huge difference between Damien (bad George) and Scoopie (good George).

"Scoopie is good and kind," she said. "He saved the life of a sheepdog about to run out into two-way traffic. He helps little old ladies and breaks up fights on the street. He buys me candles, Jelly Bellys, Rice Krispie Treats, and expensive toilet paper. He tells me I'm pretty. He's thoughtful about calling and e-mailing. Whenever he introduces me to someone new, I can always tell they've heard good stuff about me. It's a huge confidence booster. He takes me out to fancy restaurants and commiserates when I have problems at work. He's very polite and gallant, paying for dinner, the way boys are supposed to be, but never were with me. It's so sweet. Most important, he makes me laugh."

"How does he make you laugh, Hilly?"

"Anytime I ask him to do an accent, any accent, it comes out Scottish. It's hysterical!" she said, laughing. "Then there are the malaprops: 'Reese's penis.' 'The Wolling Stones.' So many more. It happens almost every day! But the best are the Milky Ways, a term I came up with. It's when you get a buildup of saliva stuck in the back of your throat, usually brought on by something like syrupy foods, ginger ale, milk, Starbursts, certain things. It's a mystery. But it distorts your voice so you sound like a munchkin. It sometimes happens to George when he's being very serious, Mr. Grownup, and it's impossible for me to contain myself, which makes him furious. But then he starts laughing, too."

"I see. What else makes him a laugh riot?"

"He eats everything out of a large soup tureen with a ladle, even pasta! He wears red cowboy pajamas, UGG boots, and walks to the corner store in his bathrobe with two different shoes. He looks ridiculous! And so cute! And I love his 'inventions.' He thinks he came up with the idea of biting the bottom of an ice cream cone and sucking the ice cream through it. And that he coined the word *ding-dong*, meaning a 'buffoon.' The best was his 'bath pillow,' which was literally a down-filled pillow that he submerged in a full bathtub, and then he was shocked to discover it molding a few days later."

Dr. Selman had not yet cracked a smile.

"He sits around the apartment with multiple Breathe Right strips on his nose and an airplane neck pillow and drinks green tea from a flower vase. At night he sleeps with these big waxy, globby earplugs. One morning we were on our way to breakfast when he stopped on the sidewalk and stood there frozen. He said, 'Hilly, we've got a big problem—I think I found a lump!' He looked terrified and ran back to the apartment. The lump turned out to be a squishy earplug that was tangled deep in his armpit hair. He had to cut it out with scissors!"

I was grateful for the endorsements, but as usual they didn't seem to impress Dr. Selman much. So I changed the subject.

"I finally started reading *Codependent No More*," I said. "I liked some of the vignettes, but after twenty pages I began to squirm. It's so full of jargon and self-satisfaction. I don't want to turn into one of those Recovery People and become a proselytizing bore. Hilly didn't do any better with it. She started nodding off. It put her to sleep. Then I turned on *Law & Order* and she perked right up."

"I wasn't in the right mood," she said.

"*Codependent No More* was missing a car chase and a murdered coed," I said. I could tell that Dr. Selman was annoyed by our flip attitude toward something he thought might help us. But he didn't show any signs of irritation and patiently explained that Hilly was the "codependent" in the relationship.

"She's the enabler who enables you not to function, to continue binge drinking, to carry on with your addiction."

"What about me?" I said. "Am I codependent?"

"The book applies more to her than you," he said. "You're on the receiving end."

I liked the sound of that. "That means it's not all my fault, right?"

"No," said Hilly. "He means I don't stand up for myself enough. I permit you to get away with too much."

"That's part of it," Dr. Selman said.

"Wait a minute," I said. "Can't I just enjoy this moment for a minute? Bask in the knowledge that I'm not the evildoer?"

"Well, it takes two to tango," he said.

"I often feel like I'm responsible not just for her emotional well-being, but too many of her emotions," I said. "It's like I'm her mood regulator. So it's good that she's being more independent."

Dr. Selman shook his head. "I think it's the opposite. Hilly's much more responsible for your emotional well-being than you are for hers. I might add that to the extent you are ill-tempered, it's rooted in depression and made worse by alcohol. If you want to improve your moods and reduce your level of irritability, you ought to give up booze, abstain from late nights out in the company of floozies, and try medication."

But my visceral antipathy to antidepressants had been reinforced by observation of Hilly and her Prozac trances. So once again I rebuffed Dr. Selman's drug offers and kept on blowing my top. Practically anything could set me off: people having brunch, the word *brunch*, people on bikes and Rollerblades, people walking too close to me on the sidewalk, people who planned ahead to score tickets to concerts and sporting events I wanted to attend but refused to plan ahead for. Overly friendly hostesses and waiters who focused on Hilly's adorable Muppet face when I was the guy shelling out the $118 plus tip. Even nonaggressive flyer distributors were capable of ruining my day.

The New York City marathon made me snarl: runners wrapped in aluminum-foil blankets, milling about, sucking fluids out of plastic bottles, limping like martyrs. "Just go home, no one cares that you did it in under six hours," I'd mutter. The German girl above me click-clacked her heels every evening. "Get some carpeting!" I'd holler at the ceiling.

For once, Dr. Selman showed some interest in my past. "Where do you think all this anger might have come from?"

I tried my best to blame it on traumatic childhood events: watching the 1972 Munich Olympics terrorist attack on television, overdosing on Charles Addams's morbid cartoons when I was a kid, a neighbor who died of a heart attack, a trip to the hospital when I swallowed some poison, a head injury from a swing-set accident, nightmares from the rock opera *Tommy*, being called Basketball Head in high school.

Dr. Selman didn't think those explained pathological anger. I groped for more convincing traumas. When I was nine, I traded a neighborhood kid two cans of Budweiser for a priceless Schmidt's cone top. Instead of letting her son learn a lesson about the sanctity of contracts, his mother rescinded the deal and I learned a lesson: the rules are made of rubber and you can't trust adults. I was tormented by bullies at boarding school. I was unfairly demoted on the tennis team and unjustly blamed for a classmate's urinating out my window onto the head of a faculty member.

"Aren't those legitimate causes for an angry mind-set?" I asked. Yes, there was no justice. Life was unfair. But as I recited these woes of childhood and adolescence, I realized how commonplace they were. They didn't excuse or explain my storming temper. I knew there was some connection between alcohol and temper. I read that anger is a drug, that chemical changes take place when you rage. And also that anger and depression go hand in hand: depression is anger turned inward. Aggression is an acquired, cathartic habit. My hatred of waiting in lines was prominently mentioned in the anger literature. I wondered if anger was one of the tactics I learned in childhood to get attention, such as the pleasure and sense of power I got from disruptive behavior in my Fonzie period.

"It sounds funny," I said. "Self-control is supposed to be the ultimate expression of power, but I sometimes feel a sense of power from losing control."

"Anger may be a response to a sense of alienation and inferiority," Dr. Selman said. "How does anger affect your life today, as an adult? What kinds of circumstances provoke it? How does it express itself?"

"Hypersensitivity to noise is one," I said. "It's something I inherited from my dad, who has a major noise phobia. I used to tell people to 'shut up' a lot and once had a lot of flare-ups over cars that invaded my space. I was crossing Fifty-Seventh and Park years ago when a car nearly clipped me. As I walked around the vehicle, I made a kicking feint. The driver jumped out, ran after me, leaped into the air, foot first, then pulled back before impact. He called me 'Faggot!' and I threw a tube of ChapStick at him."

"So both of you were out of control," said Dr. Selman.

"He's big on mimicking people who annoy him," Hilly said. "We were in a Blockbuster store the other day. George started to imitate a guy talking loudly on his cell phone: 'Oh, really, that's sooo fascinating! You're going to visit friends in Amherst this weekend? Driving up there in your Prius? Picking up some organic . . . vegetables . . . at the store? Oh, reeeeeeealy? I didn't know shiitake mushrooms are an aphrodisiac!'

"Another time, we were in line at Duane Reade when some scrawny guy was talking about a 'deal,' throwing seven figures around, and practicing his golf swing. George went, 'Do you think anyone wants to hear about your pathetic million-dollar Internet deal? That's some real fuck-you money! I'm sure Bill Gates is wetting his khakis and V-neck sweater. Is there really someone on the other end of the line or is it your imaginary friend? Are there even batteries in there?' People look at him like he's crazy, but they usually do shut up."

"She thinks it's funny," I said. "And I get a rush out of it." But I was beginning to realize that I was playing with fire and that someday I was going to get my payback. The first sign might have been when I was crossing Second Avenue one day in the late nineties. I was on my way to the dry cleaner's, my arms full of shirts and pants, when a BMW lurched forward and blocked my way. I tapped the hood of the car with my umbrella, somewhere between a tap and a smack. The female driver screamed at me, turned on the hazard lights, got out of the car, and ran. Confident of my righteousness, I shrugged it off and entered the dry cleaner's. A few moments later, out the window, I saw the driver with a policeman in tow. After I dropped off my laundry, I sauntered off in the opposite direction, zipped around the corner, then sped up.

"There he is!" the woman cried. A chase ensued. She and the cop were gasping when they caught up with me outside Gourmet Garage.

"I don't know what she's talking about, she almost hit me," I said.

"Well, she said you scratched her car." The three of us went back to survey the "damage." She pointed to scratches on the front, the sides, the bumpers, everywhere.

"How could I have done all that with my hands full of clothes?" I asked.

"I want you to arrest him because he's a psycho!" she said. Fortunately, the lady's driver's license had expired. "I'm going to file a complaint," she hissed as she made her retreat. That episode ended in a draw, but I felt giddy with victory. I wanted to high-five the cop. It didn't dawn on me that my knack for confrontations was bringing me into hazardous proximity to the law. Someday I was going to wax wroth with the wrong person and get a knife in my neck.

The dawn of enlightenment arrived one night at a Mafia-owned bar in Kansas City. After I'd won at pool, I took a bathroom break. At the next urinal a young man began to ridicule my "gay" shirt and tie.

"If that guy keeps on taunting me, I'm going to pummel him with a pool cue," I said when I returned.

"Nahhh," said my friend Hampton. "You don't want to do that."

"Why not?"

"Paperwork."

"Paperwork?"

"Yeah, as in the police will show up and it'll turn into a hassle involving lots of paperwork."

"Paperwork, huh?"

"Paperwork."

It had a Zen-like clarity, though I failed to fully appreciate its significance at the time. Less than a year later I learned about paperwork the hard way. I was on a train heading home for the holidays. Halfway to Kansas City, there was a seven-hour delay after a car ran into the train. When we finally made it to the station, I waited in line for four hours to get a hotel voucher.

The next day, I stopped by customer service and the lady behind the counter snapped at me to go wait in line some more. After what I'd been through (eleven-hour delay; freezing cold; no heat, food, or sleep on the train), I thought I'd earned some politeness, if not special attention, or just a smile. She barked at me again. I responded with an inappropriate remark and made a playful gesture of sweeping her coffee cup off the table. The next thing I knew, I was escorted away by the police. I spent a freezing night in jail trying to use my loafers as a pillow and had the leisure of quite a few wakeful hours in which to focus my thoughts. I eventually got off with an apology to the woman I'd offended. I said I was sorry, that she was just doing her job, and I hoped she'd see it in her heart to forgive me. My lawyer advised me that I was lucky to have emerged unscathed from that jail cell. Back home, Peter Stevenson, my longtime *Observer* editor and mentor, said I'd been given "a warning from the universe." I told Dr. Selman that this experience had really changed my life.

"It was a wake-up call," I said. "I was terrified. And for the first time I understood that anger was the enemy of my welfare. Since then, whenever I've felt rage coming on, I've experienced a visceral nausea. A surfer-dude voice in my head whispers, 'Stay cool. Don't give in to this pressure. You don't need an adrenaline rush now. It's not a life-or-death situation. It's just a fool on his BlackBerry and you're mellowwwwwww, neither a vicious baboon nor a lowly British civil servant getting walked on by an officious superior. Relaaaaax. Don't give in. You're in a Jamaica of the mind and here comes some Jimmy Cliff on the jukebox. You can see clearly now. All those obstacles in your way? Just blow them gently away. They're phantoms. We're not even gonna fantasize about hurling invectives at the BlackBerry twerp. Not worth it. Chillll. Remember, "paperwork." Avoid paperwork at all costs. Feel that toxin going away? Your fight-or-flight system's in cool-down mode. See? It's shutting down.'"

"It sounds as if you're learning," Dr. Selman said. "Actually, you're using a form of cognitive behavioral therapy."

That made me feel good. I was beginning to understand that I needed to master some of these problems on my own. No one, including your shrink, can do it for you. I remember sitting next to an old man coughing his lungs out on a bench in downtown Lawrence, Kansas, and asking him for some advice before I returned to the big city. "Find out for yourself!" he growled.

CHAPTER FOURTEEN

MONEY MATTERS

Dr. Selman first got the idea we had financial problems when I told him I was going to have to postdate his check. He asked for a little clarification. That simple question unlocked a torrent of confessional self-pity.

"I'm thirty-seven years old and I have ten dollars in the bank," I said. "I can't plan ahead. I wait until the last moment to buy a plane ticket, which doubles the cost. I'm in a dead-end job." Writing for a newspaper gave me a veneer of success. But I felt stagnant. Newspaper readership was in decline. I could foresee the day when I might lose my job. I let such morose speculations excuse me from producing stories, which inspired my bosses to cut my salary in half and somehow convince me it was a promotion.

Why hadn't I listened to my father? A journalist himself, he thought the profession was doomed. "Join the ministry, the army," he said. "Start a Laundromat or become a pastry chef in Portugal. Something with a future. Otherwise, you'll end up operating a leaf blower or delivering pizzas."

I gave him a typically impudent reply. "My ambition is to make enough money to buy a brand-new pair of tube socks every day and throw them away every night." Now, even that luxury seemed to be slipping out of reach.

I'd thought about business school and spent a thousand dollars on tutors for the GMAT, but I had no idea what I would do with a degree. I whiled away hours in semicomatose nostalgia, daydreaming about moving back to my college town, renting that same one-room studio for $300 a month, getting my old dishwashing job at the microbrewery, auditing classes, and pursuing other undirected studies. The first time this bright idea came up in therapy, Dr. Selman asked if I'd ever seen *The Twilight Zone* episode "Hooverville."

"It's about a guy who falls asleep on a train and wakes up in his hometown," he said. Apparently, some ironic subtext was intended. Was the doctor suggesting I was an escapist? And what if the dream came true and I really did wake up down-and-out in Lawrence, Kansas? I'd probably become another local oddity like the guy who walks in the middle of the street dressed only in a dirty sheet, holding his hands before him, playing an invisible piano.

I spent hours badgering editors for raises and whining about my desperate circumstances.

"You're not being tough enough," Hilly said. "You have to bully your bosses." She recommended reading *You Can Negotiate Anything*. "You have to come at them with a crowbar. Threaten them with cement shoes."

"Let's talk about changes that you could make in the here and now," said Dr. Selman. "Anything you could do besides running away and becoming a busboy?"

I vented a torrent of excuses. "Reporting is a young man's job. My insides are already annihilated. I've developed breathing problems and heart palpitations. I've got asthma. Can't you hear my wheeze? Maybe I could start over and go back to fact-checking. Or write a book! Of course, that would take forever. I'd spend two years writing it. It would sell at the most five thousand copies. Great! Then I'd be broke again."

Hilly had had some bright ideas of her own. "I've thought about selling my eggs. That could make us ten thousand dollars. But I'd have to quit drinking. I tried bartending, but I quit when the boss told me about the initiation: I'd have to have sex with all the male employees. I thought it was a joke until one of the other employees asked for help reading the time on his watch. I looked down at his wrist and saw he was having trouble because his penis was in the way. I told the boss. He said that if I didn't like the job, I could always quit."

That anecdote left Dr. Selman speechless for a couple of beats. He abandoned the subject of job opportunities and turned to issues of thrift. "Do you two ever discuss ways to cut expenses?"

The truth about our expensive dining habits came out. "We go out to dinner every night we're together," I said. "Places that cost one hundred and twenty dollars, minimum, the way she orders wine."

"Why not try dining at home?" he said.

"He expects me to whip up breakfast every morning," said Hilly. "Scrambled eggs with caviar and gravlax—in bed."

"She can't cook," I said. "I was sick for days after eating her chicken and dumplings."

"Who pays for these extravagant dinners?" Dr. Selman asked.

"I do, always," I said, expecting to receive praise for myself and a rebuke for Hilly.

He disappointed me. "Well, that's how things work. The

boy pays." How could he say that in this day and age? Once again, I felt betrayed.

"Hilly's salary is twice mine," I said.

"But you're the man," Hilly chirped, beaming with self-righteousness. "The woman has upkeep expenses a man doesn't have. Cosmetics, highlights, clothes, high heels."

"She has one hundred and fifty pairs of Manolos and Louboutins," I said. "Those are essentials."

"And don't forget about shoe repairs, stockings, and so on," she said. "And hundreds of dollars a month for basic hair maintenance."

"Why so much?" said Dr. Selman, obviously impressed.

"It's expensive to be blond in New York City," said Hilly with a toss of her luminous hair. Then she craftily snuck in another theme. "Things might change if we were legally bound. Maybe a joint checking account would help." I was wise to that gambit. It was another sneak attack in the campaign to put a collar around my neck and march me to the pillory of wedlock. I countered with my own non sequitur.

"After four years of dating, would it violate decorum if 'the woman' sprung for the occasional taxi or movie?"

"Have you ever thought about changing your habit of staying out all night?" said Dr. Selman, executing a perfect ninety-degree change of subject. "That could lead to more alertness, more wakeful hours the following day. You might find that it enhanced your ability to concentrate on writing. That could lead to increased productivity. And more money."

I had no answer to that. How do you argue the opposite side of basic common sense? The fact was, I didn't want common sense. I wanted alibis.

CHAPTER FIFTEEN

THE PROMISE RING

"I want to slow things down." That was my favorite theme in our sessions with Dr. Selman. "I want to hit reset before we march forward into the unknown." I understood it was time to put away childish things, that youth was behind me, that irresponsibility and promiscuity were inappropriate to my age, and that the settled life made sense rationally, as well as health-wise. But the words of Al Goldstein, publisher of *Screw* magazine, kept coming back to me: "Death Before Marriage!" Wedding bells signaled the end of freedom, possibilities, surprise, renewal, and joy, and condemnation to a sleepwalking, moribund demilife.

Hilly, on the other hand, had her sights set on connubial bliss. She was subtle, crafty about it—but the goal was always there. One of her strategies was to interject the subject of babies into our conversations, no matter how irrelevant. Everything she wanted had a "baby" in it. She longed for a baby Scottie dog, a little baby cheeseburger, a baby bite of mashed potatoes.

"It's her favorite word," I told Dr. Selman. "She calls things babies that aren't babies. 'When you go to Union Market, won't you get me one of those little baby cupcakes?'"

"You do it, too," said Hilly. "When I caught you drunk with those two floozies in Siberia, you called me 'baby.' Remember? 'Don't worry, baby. Everything's gonna be all right.'"

"That wasn't the same thing," I grumbled.

"You like to hold Baba like she's a little baby," Hilly said. "And you refer to yourself as her 'mama,' and you wrapped her up in a pair of your tighty-whities so she looked like the Baby Jesus in swaddling clothes."

"That doesn't mean I want to have babies."

"I'm on birth control," Hilly said to set the record straight. "I was against the idea, but now I'm happy about it."

In my mind, the subtext of her baby talk, of course, was commitment, engagement, and marriage. Sometimes, probably just to taunt me, she sang, "Love and marriage . . . go together like a horse and carriage." She particularly liked to hit me with a chorus of that song when I was trying to coax her into an amorous mood. I wasn't rabidly hostile to the message, just wary. I recognized that by age forty, you're in prison whether married or single. And there were good points to consider. Marriage might encourage a flowering of personal responsibility and even morality. People might start thinking of me as a gentleman, instead of a dissipated party boy. Besides, something about debauchery at my age was pathetic. I knew it was good for me to be in a relationship, however unstable. I could even imagine a little Hilly—just not a little George. But I was completely unprepared for marriage talk. Words such as *wedding ring*, *set a date*, *vows*, and *best man* gave me the williwaws.

For once, Dr. Selman was on my side. I concluded it was

because he thought Hilly was nuts even to consider marrying me. I could imagine him standing up at our wedding when the preacher asks, "If any man can show any just cause why they may not lawfully be joined together, speak now or forever hold your peace." When Hilly told him about finding me in the bathroom at Siberia with the two floozies, he was disappointed that she thought it was funny.

"Why do you put up with this behavior?" he said.

"I love George. He makes me laugh. He said that they needed a place to stay and that he'd invited them over."

"I don't understand how you can find this amusing," said Dr. Selman.

"One of his big points was that they like French toast, just like I do," she said. "It was no big deal. My main complaint was that George didn't call me when he said he would. And what had he been doing for three hours?"

"Chatting with two drunk floozies in the bathroom," said Dr. Selman.

"I was working," I said. "Wires got crossed. Plans changed. Confusion ensued. One thing led to another and I wound up in the bathroom with Olsen twin look-alikes."

"They're cute, actually," said Hilly. "Friendly. Funny little monkeys."

"I can't believe you're giving him a pass," said Dr. Selman.

"It is insulting that he'd rather spend time with them than me," said Hilly.

"I'd rather be with you," I said, attempting to change the subject. "Hilly's my guardian angel." I told him about the time we were together late at Dorothy's when Dave Attell, the comedian, started hurling insults at me. "Hilly came to my rescue. She actually lunged at him and peppered him with expletives."

"I'm sick and tired of people being obnoxious to him," said Hilly. "But I don't like it when he's out late and I don't know where he is. What if he's dead?"

Dr. Selman tried to refocus the conversation. "I've been meaning to ask you guys something. Do you think of yourselves as a monogamous couple?"

"Yes! *Of course,*" Hilly almost bellowed.

"Yeah," I said after a pregnant pause.

"Where do you want the relationship to go?" he asked.

"Status quo," I said.

"What does that mean?" said Dr. Selman.

"Yeah," Hilly added. "What does that mean?"

"I don't know. Maybe keep things right where they are for now? I'm not sure taking it to the next level is the wise thing to do, so why not make a lateral move, try to work things out, and then see what happens?"

"Where do you think the relationship is heading?" Dr. Selman asked Hilly.

"I can't imagine breaking up with Georgie. Or life without him. I'd hate it if he weren't my boyfriend. I don't know what I'd do. Before we even discuss marriage, I think we both need to grow up, be in more control of our lives, emotionally and financially. Once we do that, it would be a nice thing to do down the road."

"What about you?" said Dr. Selman. "Is marriage a possibility?"

"Let's not get ahead of ourselves," I said. "A day at a time. The fact is I'm here, right now, in therapy with my girlfriend. So obviously I want things to improve."

But the marriage issue persisted. During one session, I returned from a visit to the restroom to find Hilly holding forth about her fantasy wedding.

"My plan has always been to keep it small," she was saying. "Not a big to-do. Not too much of a show. I'd want to go somewhere like the Seychelles or the Maldives for the honeymoon, me and whoever it is I'm marrying. I would need a beautiful dress by Oscar de la Renta, not a wedding dress, just something I can wear again. And maybe a small cocktail reception would be nice, with family members and a few close friends."

"'Whoever it is I'm marrying'?" I said. "What's that supposed to mean?" It sounded like a warning. The two of them were conspiring against me again, hatching schemes without any input from me.

"Have you asked George to marry you, officially?" Dr. Selman asked.

"More or less. Not really. No," Hilly said.

"I keep reminding her to honor what I said the second night we met: that I'd never get married before forty. Besides, shouldn't we be working on our financial problems and drinking habits before we start talking about engagement rings?"

"By the way," said Dr. Selman. "You might consider taking Hilly to the Fairmont Copley Plaza in Boston. For about fifteen hundred dollars you can order a martini there that comes with a one-carat engagement ring."

"I'd be happy with something from Harry Winston or Verdura," Hilly said. "I don't want something that came from a Cracker Jack box. I was against the idea of living together before getting married, but I think I might consider it if I got a ring."

"I'd like to bring up the subject of the rent, which I'm not presently capable of paying."

"You know, an engagement can be called off easily," said Hilly. "You don't even need a lawyer. You just take off the ring, shake hands, say good-bye. You go your separate ways and stay friends. It's really easy."

Dr. Selman offered a perverse argument to dissuade Hilly from thinking of me as marriage material. "Have you ever thought that you might not like George as much if he mended his ways?"

"He's not really the maverick he pretends to be," said Hilly. "He actually likes to be told what to do. Wash the dishes. Pick up my dry cleaning. Clean up his room. The problem is I've had no experience at this. I'm terrible at delegating or being an authority figure."

The discussion often seemed designed to humiliate me, but I let it go. I had my own strategy, and it was this: if I could keep the chatter about rings and marriage going in inane circles, I might not get cornered and forced to act. Talking about the subject seemed to have a therapeutic effect on Hilly. It might serve to dissipate the pressure and save me from having to step into the quicksand. But that stratagem was blown out of the water the night when Hilly came over to my apartment for "Christmas Exchange." That's the Xmas ritual for loved ones who aren't related, she explained.

"We can exchange presents on any day in December except the twenty-fifth," she said. She was well acquainted with my phobia for "gifts" and was hoping to avoid an ugly scene by giving me utilitarian items devoid of sentimental nuance. She brought in tow a cargo of identically wrapped boxes. Grimly, I started unwrapping. In the first box I found a pair of boxer shorts from the Gap. I rewarded her with my idea of gift-recipient etiquette.

"Just what I wanted." I opened the second box. Another pair of boxer shorts, these from Brooks Brothers with the monogram GG. A linen number from Barneys followed.

"I'm picking up on an undergarment motif," I said.

"There are lots of them. Thirty, to be exact."

"Okay, I get the picture. I'll open the rest of them later."

"There's something else." She handed me a smaller package. I opened it: notebooks. Dozens of them, from a fifty-cent Mead pad to an elegant Smythson diary. I stopped opening. For months packages of boxers and notebooks would be around the apartment with only one corner of wrapping paper torn off, the ribbons still tied around them. Finally one day Hilly unwrapped them herself and put them neatly away.

Without ceremony, I gave Hilly her present, a bottle of Veuve Clicquot. She didn't complain about its being wrapped in a plastic bag. Christmas Exchange wasn't over, though. It turned out that the mundane gifts were a ploy designed to soften me up.

"There's something I want to talk to you about," she said in a stern, grown-up tone. "It's really not a big deal but it would mean an awful lot to me."

"You want to have sex?"

She gave me a pleading look. "I'd like to have a ring."

"A ring?" I nearly screamed.

"Please, please, please, just give me this one thing without making a big deal out of it."

"No," I muttered.

She started crying. "I just feel like it would be a nice token of commitment, after so long. It would make me feel better on those nights when you're out so late and I'm thinking you're probably going to jump into the arms of some hussy."

"Hilly, you don't have to worry about that. So what is this ring? Is it a friendship ring?"

"No!"

"A pre-engagement ring?"

"A promise ring. That's all I want. And if you don't give it to me, then it's over."

"No." I considered the case closed and was pleased with my judicial restraint. But I'd misjudged my adversary. Hilly jumped up and stormed out of the apartment in tears. I waited for an hour. Finally I called her and I talked her down.

"Is everything okay then?" I said.

"So does that mean you'll give me the ring?"

I said no a third time. I could hear another wave of sobbing.

"Well, then, good-bye forever!" she said, and hung up. It was the first time she'd stood up to me. I was shocked. I felt terrible. I panicked. My swaggering, free-spirit persona collapsed. The next day I capitulated and agreed to her terms and presented her with the ring on the corner of Fifth Avenue. She admitted to being a "teeny, tiny bit hurt" that it was unwrapped and that the inscription I'd chosen didn't incorporate the word *love*. But she was elated.

"You two are engaged?" Dr. Selman asked when the subject of the ring came out. "Don't you think that's something I should know? So what exactly does the ring mean?"

"It's a promise ring," Hilly said. "And it wasn't even his idea. After three years I thought it would be nice to have something to look at to make myself feel better."

"When I go out, she always pictures me frolicking with other girls. When she asked for a promise ring, I instinctively said no, which made her cry. I tried to calm her down. Nothing worked. After she threatened to break up with me, I got her one."

"I thought it would be a nice token of commitment!"

"That was when I suspected she was plotting to get married, have kids," I said. "She asked for a ring. I said no. She started crying, I said maybe. She threatened to break up with me, so I got her one."

"He's forgetting to tell you how I didn't answer or return

his desperate calls for five days. I *needed* that token of commitment. I had to have it for my sense of pride. After almost three years I was being hounded with questions from my friends and family about our relatioship. I thought this would be a good start."

"So the ring means you're . . . ," Dr. Selman said.

"Almost engaged," said Hilly.

"It's not an engagement ring!" I cried.

"Pre-engaged."

"Sort of engaged."

CHAPTER SIXTEEN

A WEEK IN ROME...
AND FEAR OF FLYING

Hilly had to go to Rome for some corporate training for her new job. She needed to meet one-on-one with colleagues in the home office as well as some of her global counterparts. It would be a stressful week for her, so I decided to come along in support.

Besides the all-expenses-paid weekend in D.C., we'd had several family-related vacations together (Kansas, Ohio, Florida). But this would be our first real trip, just the two of us, and it coincided with our fifth anniversary. One huge plus was that Hilly spoke fluent Italian. I dreamed of dashing through the Eternal City, tossing coins into the Trevi Fountain, and sticking my hand into the Mouth of Truth just as Gregory Peck and Audrey Hepburn did in *Roman Holiday. Meraviglioso!*

While Hilly was at work, I'd have freedom to sightsee and search for a new identity. She'd scored a room at the Hotel Eden, one of the best in the world. I'd be wallowing in luxury.

I'd walk on cobblestones that Julius Caesar's feet had touched. *"Volare!"* I thought. *"Veni, vidi, vici* and *cin cin."* The only worries that lay before me were in the promise I made to Hilly to show her how much she meant to me on the Spanish Steps and my paralyzing fear of flying.

Halfway to Rome, the Heinekens weren't calming me down, especially after the pilot announced with a casual drawl that we were about to pick up some "light chop." I needed Demerol to make it across the Atlantic. I tried reciting the mantra "Even though I have a fear of flying, I accept myself profoundly and completely." But the inner voice erupted in mocking laughter and reminded me that while boarding I'd forgotten to put my right hand on the plane and bless it. "Now you're scared," it said. "You don't accept yourself and you're seconds away from blazing death." I tried some other palliatives: "Every minute ten planes are taking off and ten are landing. . . . It's like being on a ship and the air outside is like waves. . . . The wingtips will touch each other before they fall off. . . . The pilot doesn't want to die, he's got the right stuff, and what makes me so special that my plane will go down and I'll meet a fiery demise?"

On the TV screen in front of me, a quote from Robert Louis Stevenson appeared: "For my part, I travel not to go anywhere, but to go. I travel for travel's sake. The great affair is to move." Somehow that, along with a second Xanax, chilled me out. With heart rate and breathing back to normal, I decided I wanted something major to happen in Rome: a religious experience, an epiphany, a vision. Maybe I'd receive the stigmata. I might have some carnal pleasures, too. As I was finally drifting off, Hilly began to worry that I'd meet an Italian woman and leave her.

"How can I meet any if I'm going to be with you the whole

time?" I asked while images of Gina Lollobrigida and Sophia Loren sauntered through my mind.

At last, we landed. Still alive. Hilly showed off her Italian to the cabdriver, who whisked us to the Eden. Our $800-a-night room wasn't ready yet so we had breakfast and an argument at the rooftop restaurant.

"I'm ready for a real drink," she said.

"No," I said. "Too early. Coke Lights and cigarettes are as far as I'm going to let you go." Now that we were back on terra firma, a new fear arose. This trip would ruin us financially. When the breakfast turned out to be complimentary, I felt a little better. Once inside our room, I passed out for five hours, until Hilly began running her hair dryer, slamming drawers, and whistling. I begged her to leave me in peace. She waited for me in the lobby and cried.

When I rejoined her, we went out into the aromatic Roman air. Down the Spanish Steps we danced, which reminded me of my Valentine's Day promise to take our relationship to the next level. Hell, after four years, I'd only said the three magic words the first time we had sex and "I heart you" another time I was drunk. Time to rectify that and redeem myself. We got a table at Caffè Greco. It was crowded, noisy, and not dark enough for me. The waiters looked as if they'd been there since it opened in 1760. They ignored us. I threatened to bolt. Hilly transformed herself into an aggressive Italian and demanded service. We got service, but the waiter brought us pastries rather than the pasta Hilly had ordered. I was becoming agitated. I couldn't take the wait for the check, so Hilly paid it and found me on the Via dei Condotti.

It started to drizzle as I tried to find the Pantheon. Soon we were lost. Knowing I was in a weakened, vulnerable state, Hilly didn't ask for directions, roll her eyes, or say the "wrong" thing, which might have caused a blowup or breakdown and set the tone for the whole trip. Pretty much any utterance could achieve that, even a gentle white lie like "Don't worry, Scoopie, we'll get there, you're doing a great job."

We changed directions a half dozen times. My confidence drooped. Hilly became more reticent. I sensed frustration brewing. She was there for work. Her free time was minimal. And her boneheaded boyfriend was about to get into one of his foul moods. Just then we stumbled upon our destination. We both stared in awe at the two-thousand-year-old temple. Inside it, I got an odd sensation. The dome, which had a hole in the top, seemed to me like a monumental embodiment of my head. Except that, according to what I'd read, it was a miracle of proportion.

I got us lost again on the way to the Campo dei Fiori. This time Hilly got some assistance from a shopkeeper, who was thrilled to help an Italian-speaking tourist. Back on the right path with a map, she managed to find the Piazza Navona. The last time I was in Rome, I was barked at by local carabiniere when I attempted to commandeer a local's Vespa and take it on a spin around the ancient course where chariots once raced. Hilly didn't want to hear about it. She wanted a drink.

Hilly seemed distant, mute. She was slipping into Inner Hilly World. Whenever this metamorphosis occurred, it puzzled and scared me. She was supposed to be the Rock of Gibraltar, my mood regulator, my Prozac, and I always had to know exactly what she was thinking to feel okay about myself. As the seconds of silence ticked away, I started to panic. I had to force some kind of reaction, to coax some comforting words from her—or to make her mad.

So I started in.

"Is everything all right?" Silence. "Are you mad at me?"

"No."

"Are you sure?"

"Yes."

"Are you tired of me asking that?"

"No."

"Okay, but are you mad at me now?"

"No." Pause. "Yes!"

Good. Now I had what I needed. I apologized and felt a wave of relief and calm wash over me. At last she was communicating. As usual, a quaff of wine revived her spirits, too.

Back at the Eden, she gave me permission to nap. This time her crying woke me up. Eddie, her neighbor in the West Village, had called with some bad news: a notice for eviction was on her front door and the locks had been changed. Hilly called the rental office, sobbing and arguing, then begging for mercy. No dice. She was late with the rent again and already owed a few grand. She reminded Bernard, the landlord, that she had been a good tenant for eleven years and didn't sue about the toxic mold, so couldn't they work something out? She thought she had an agreement with Alexandra. Sorry, Bernard said. Alexandra didn't work there anymore. It was too late.

Hilly started screaming after hanging up. I handed her half a Xanax, then called our friend Tracy, who put us in touch with his flamboyant real estate and civil rights attorney, Tommy Shanahan, who got on the case. Within an hour he determined that the owners of Hilly's building were "scum lords" notorious for evicting blind, deaf, elderly women who'd been living in their apartments for decades—as well as young, privileged blondes who'd naively informed the rental office they were traveling overseas. That's when they'd strike. They wanted Hilly out so they could renovate and charge five times more for rent. She went to pieces when she heard that all her stuff might be put in storage and her cat, Svenny, dumped in a shelter. I tried to put a good spin on the situation: everyone gets evicted once. It's no big deal, it's a rite of passage in New York, plus it didn't matter because we were in Rome. Things happen for a reason. This is all a blessing in disguise. Let's get out of here now. Dinnertime. Drinks.

We left. Walking down the Via Veneto I tried to steady and distract her with talk of la dolce vita. I found a restaurant and, as soon as we were seated, ordered white wine. The sommelier poured the wine with a flourish. The waiter hovered over us like a benevolent father.

"I bet he has hair coming out of his ears," said Hilly, referring to her landlord. "I bet he has dandruff and combs his chest hair into crescent shapes." Although patrons were looking over at us now, I thought it was worth it. It was therapeutic for Hilly to rant. "I bet he was fat and geeky as a kid and always got picked last for dodgeball. I bet he hasn't been laid since age twenty-one."

Eventually the tempest subsided and Hilly got up to use the ladies' room. I fell into a pensive mood. I wanted that peak experience, and all I was getting was bile about Bernard. When she returned, dinner was served. It looked like something heated up in a microwave. Hilly couldn't touch her food. "Oh, what am I going to do?" she moaned. She smiled at the waiter who laid down the check: 130 euros.

We stopped at the Hotel Excelsior. In the near-empty ballroom, Hilly played a sad version of "Chopsticks" on the grand piano. She was down, big-time. To preempt another outburst, I ordered champagne. All of a sudden she cheered up. The eviction disaster presented her with a golden opportunity: she would have to move in with me. That triggered another of my phobias: cohabitation. I mumbled something about "for the time being" and "until you find another place." I let her fantasize about how great it would be having two closets now (once we moved Baba's litter box into the kitchen) and her own bed-room, once I moved into the cubbyhole alcove "upstairs."

Back at our hotel, her mood took another nosedive. After she made a "joke" about how romantic it would be to throw herself into the Tiber, I called Dr. Selman, who talked her down and doubled her meds. She asked if anyone had ever been prescribed that much outside of an institution. He said eighty milligrams was kosher and advised Hilly not to let anything ruin her vacation. He thought she might even score a big settlement with the landlord.

"It worked one time for me," he said. Lastly, he made her recite the Serenity Prayer.

Next Tommy the lawyer called to say he might be able to delay things, prevent the confiscation of her possessions, and, yes, a buyout was possible. Then there was good news this time from Eddie the neighbor, who said he'd sneaked into her apartment through the fire-escape window and rescued Svenny. We slept close to each other, arms entwined, and when I woke up, Hilly was gone.

She had two morning appointments. The first was a visit to a company workshop where craftsmen create multimillion-dollar pieces of high-end jewelry. Then it was off to meet a gemologist, who led her into the vault that housed her com-pany's archival collection of jewels.

While I was trying in vain to find the Trevi Fountain and the chapel with the Caravaggios, Hilly was getting dizzy from seeing, handling, and trying on priceless jewels from the far ends of the earth, among them the Seven Wonders necklace with more than a hundred carats of rare Colombian emeralds.

We connected for lunch, then got our caricatures drawn in the Piazza Navona, drawing an audience of idle gawk-ers. Hilly's portrait was flattering. While the artist created a ghastly portrait of me, a little boy kept whispering into the ear of his mother, who shook her head and scolded him. "I think he's saying you look like his crazy uncle Fredo," Hilly said.

She went back to work and I napped for the rest of the day. On the way to dinner that evening, Tommy called with bad news. All of her stuff would be hauled away and placed in storage the following day.

"Everything's fine, don't worry, this was meant to happen," I said in a *che sarà* voice. Hilly was inconsolable. She kept moving, staring straight ahead, saying nothing until we crossed a street and a car got too close. Then she exploded in rage, filling the Roman air with expletives, first English, then Italian: *"Roba da matti! Rompo le gambe!"*

At a five-hundred-year-old restaurant, Hilly listed some of her treasured, soon-to-be-seized possessions: "My stuffed animals, Piggie, who I've had since I was eight. My teddy, Bear Huxtable; Le Mutt, the puppy you got me in Kansas; Marcel the prairie dog and Scruffy the sea lion from San Francisco. One hundred and fifty pairs of Manolos, family heirlooms, books about Jackie O, a bottle of Stoli in the lowboy fridge, my treasure box. My memory bowl. Pierre's ashes. Granny Bee's pillbox-hat collection. Cary Berryman's wedding bouquet between my mattress and box spring. And my witchcraft handbooks." Then she cursed Bernard some more.

"The girls at the corner deli call him the Egg Man because he smells like a rotten egg," she said. "The only reason I was evicted was so that he could get into my apartment, sniff my panties, and sell Svenny to Hunan Park." She vowed to send him a box of dead cockroaches and bewitch him with *malocchio*, the evil eye. *"Ti rompo le gambe."*

I was beginning to wonder if she had really acquired some expertise from those witchcraft books. One thing was certain:

Dispensing curses went a lot better in Italian than English. She sounded as if she meant it, and that whatever spell she was casting was going to work. It scared me a bit. I began to feel sorry for Bernard. And myself, because there weren't any prices on the menu. More visions of bankruptcy.

"I love when they do that, it's so chic," Hilly said. "I can probably expense it."

After I paid the check (180 euros), we went to the Bulldog Inn, an international bar where I'd gotten into trouble a decade earlier. I met a nice young Austrian girl that night, and when her date left for the men's room, I suggested she meet me at the bar the next afternoon. Astrid nodded enthusiastically, so I'm pretty sure she understood me. As soon as she left, I decided to celebrate early (gonna have an affair starting tomorrow!) and woke up the next day with a hangover, made worse by the realization that I'd slept through my tryst.

Inside the Bulldog, Hilly and I pounded drinks and mocked the "cheesy Euro lame-os" (her phrase), who were singing along to nineties hits including Chumbawamba's "Tubthumping," "Zombie" by the Cranberries, and "What's Up?" by 4 Non Blondes. After last call, I persuaded three Italian guys to drive us to a nightclub. Hilly was against the idea but piled into the back, and the guys dropped us off somewhere twenty minutes away. There, I realized that my wallet was gone. In the Bulldog bathroom? Backseat? No idea. We made it back to the Eden by dawn. Suddenly, my carefree, "go with the flow" attitude, the same one I'd been recommending to Hilly, was gone.

When normal, responsible people travel overseas and go out drinking, they bring some cash along, traveler's checks, and a photocopy of their passport. They leave their wallet and other valuables in the room safe, not by a bathroom window in a bar. And if they do lose their wallet, it's at the hands of a pickpocket, a street urchin, a Gypsy, a maid, or at gunpoint. Why wasn't I normal?

I remembered a strange, swarthy young man at the Bulldog. He had a Polaroid and kept insisting we needed pictures taken of us. Then I handed him ten euros . . . out of my wallet. Hilly wasn't helping. Rather than talk me out of this downward spiral, she began jabbering all kinds of nonsense about identity theft: "Not to be a Debbie Downer, Scoops, but you're wasting your time. If I were you, I'd be at the American embassy right now. You can't mess around with these criminals—they'll destroy your life!"

Although she was dead serious, she seemed to be enjoying my misfortune. "Didn't you have your new *Vanity Fair* business cards in your wallet?" she persisted. "What if they try to impersonate you? I saw an exposé on *Dateline* about a guy who lost everything he had after his credit card was stolen. You had your credit card stolen, plus your Social Security card, your insurance information, your driver's license . . . Want me to get on the FBI's website?" I ran to the bathroom and hugged the toilet and, after canceling my debit card and credit card, failed in several attempts to interest Hilly in sexual intercourse.

"Seriously, now, when your whole life is slipping out from underneath you?" she cracked. "Maybe if you take a shower." At 1:00 p.m. Hilly was looking at the room service menu.

"A club sandwich for thirty euros?" I said. "You must be kidding."

"Time for you to get out of bed," she said, yanking the covers off.

"How about you go out and get me a five-euro panino?"

She gave up on me, disappeared, and returned with a giant, inedible popover thing.

"What's with this rubbery prosciutto?" I said, gnawing at the monstrosity. "Impossible to swallow."

"Italy's for the birds," she mused. "You can never get all you need at one store."

We pulled ourselves together and somehow made it to the Protestant Cemetery—the holiest place in Rome, according to Oscar Wilde—by 4:30 p.m.

"This is where I want to spend eternity," I said. "Especially if I could get a spot near Keats or Shelley." A dozen cats were prowling around, keeping guard. We chased a few for fun. Then harp music indicated that it was closing time.

Across the street I spotted a line of unoccupied taxis by a sandwich and espresso bar. Up on a shelf were scores of brilliantly colored liquor bottles. I opted for a cold beer for the ride. When the can exploded, the driver was displeased. Hilly jabbered away in Italian, trying to explain that the spilled beer was entirely on my lap, not the backseat.

When we arrived at the Colosseum, it was closed. Hilly took it personally and fell into a funk. "This is what we get for having sinned in a past life," she said.

A three-legged kitten distracted her. She was overcome with compassion. "Kitty?" she cooed. She opined that the poor little mangy creature had been sent to us as an intercessor between us and our misfortunes. If we adopted it, our luck would change. She sent me in search of something to feed the thing. I returned with a panino, which Kitty greedily consumed. We said good-bye to little Three Legs and soon found ourselves surrounded in an enormous Hamas demonstration by the Victor Emmanuel monument. Terrorists . . . suicide bombers . . . Were these signs of the kind of fortune our rescued feline was to bring?

Back at the hotel I fell asleep in the bathtub. Hilly woke

me up and went on about how dangerous that was. We had
a reservation at the Eden's rooftop restaurant. I gave myself
a haircut, shaved between my eyebrows, while Hilly put on a
pink Luisa Beccaria dress and diamond and tourmaline Bul-
gari earrings.

"You know how you're in love with Monica Vitti?" she hol-
lered. "When I was at the vault today, I tried on the Seven
Wonders necklace that she once wore in Italian *Vogue*. I was
admiring how much I resembled her in the mirror when the
entire thing fell to the floor. Thank God it didn't crack or now
we'd really be in a hole. It's worth ten million dollars. Well,
it wasn't my fault. It's funny, at the time, I was more upset
and worried about Bernard and the marshal breaking into my
apartment, dropping my stuffed animals and abducting my
cat. . . ."

I pretended not to hear that last part, so that it wouldn't interfere with my daydream of Vitti and her brunette friend who
disappears at the beginning of *L'Avventura*. During dinner, I
had an epiphany.

"I lost my wallet, so now we're both in the same boat," I said.

"You see?" she said with frightening enthusiasm. "That
shows we're destined for one another. It makes you think that
my eviction was part of some greater plan." Back home that
would have provoked panic and an outburst, but the lights on
the street below were stunning and Hilly was glowing, too.
She looked so glamorous and happy that nothing mattered
now. I didn't object when she ordered another eighty-euro
bottle of wine. A feeling came over me I hadn't experienced
before. A kind of euphoria. One of my major fears suddenly
seemed transformed into a liberating blessing. We were going
to be living together. That sublime fact blew all our troubles
away. Later in our room, Hilly studied a picture of me as an in-

fant and said anything bad I'd ever done didn't matter because I was still the same sweet, plump little Georgie in his knickers and kneesocks.

We both passed out on the floor in the middle of *Batman Begins* and got up early to visit the Vatican. Being inside St. Peter's got me into a reformation mood. I fell into Hilly's supernatural way of interpreting misfortune. The loss of my wallet—in the same bar where I'd gotten in trouble seven years before—was an omen: my partying days were over. Everything that had happened the past two days was preordained. Real life had begun for both of us, and we were on the path to grown-up-hood.

Back to the Eden; I tried to take a nap. Hilly made that impossible by clanking bottles around in the minibar. I didn't blow my top. I had this serene, idiotic notion that I was in charge of everything from now on. A little later, in search of something to eat, we started up the Spanish Steps. Halfway to the top, Hilly stopped.

"I'm ready for that thing you promised to say and do," she said.

"Not yet," I said. "We still have thirty-six hours more in Rome." The next morning I walked her to work and returned to the Vatican Museum. During the two-hour wait in line, I thought about the forty thousand e-mails I had lost after a recent computer crash. Gone was my diary from 1997 to 2004 and the entry that read "George Gurley, you are a genius." Maybe I could get the person to resend it? "You are a fucking idiot," read another message. Wait, I printed that one out. Bad stuff never gets lost.

I also stared at the teenage girl in front of me, nubile in green corduroys and furry boots covered with hearts. Suddenly, I felt old. A stabbing pain shot through my lower back. I was tired of standing. The Sistine Chapel was overrated.

There was nowhere to sit. I saw a man with a long white beard in a wheelchair: that could be me. On the way back I stopped by the Keats museum and read one of the poet's last letters in which he said he felt dead already and was now leading a posthumous existence. I could relate to the list of his symptoms: weakness, exhaustion, general malaise, trouble breathing, swollen joints. Coughing up blood? Not yet. Rapid weight loss? More like the opposite. I left convinced my days were numbered.

Later, after a marathon shower/bubble bath, Hilly and I strolled through the Borghese gardens and watched the sunset. We rode the carousel, we headed to the Trevi Fountain. Some Gypsies accosted Hilly. She shooed them away.

"We're not in Calcutta," she yelled. Halfway up the Spanish Steps, Hilly stopped once again and waited. This was the moment of truth.

"I don't feel well," I said. "My stomach hurts. Look, there's the room where Keats died. Maybe I have tuberculosis, too."

"Not what I want to hear."

"How about this: we're going to be roommates."

"Nope, not it." She held out a hand, closed her eyes, and waited for a ring. I didn't have one. That wasn't in the Valentine's Day letter. All I did was promise to say something on the Spanish Steps.

"We sure had a great time," I said. "The trip's not over yet, and we're sure to return. We still have some hurdles to overcome."

"I promise to chip in for rent and cook supper every night."

"I'm proud of you and there's no one else I'd rather have been with in Rome. And, one more thing: I love you."

Hilly squealed with joy. Then she let loose with a cackle. "Sucker."

CHAPTER SEVENTEEN

COHABITATION

Early on in our six-year trek through couples therapy, Hilly said she would refuse to even consider cohabitation unless we were married, which she called the "M-word." According to her theory, my aversion to marriage derived from my parents' divorce when I was three years old. Their custody battle seven years later contributed to my conflicted feelings about holy matrimony. Hilly, who was thirty-one and terrified of ending up alone, harped on her parents' marriage, which was still wonderful after forty years. I told her she was lucky. My parents engaged in a hot and cold warfare, followed by icy silence. I suggested alternatives.

"Why not eventually, down the road, live together, see how that goes, maybe have a kid out of wedlock, Hollywood-style, or adopt a nice Bosnian girl who'd been left on a mountaintop? Or a pet. We could run a cat and Scottie-dog breeding farm. Aren't there enough people in the world anyway?"

Now there was no way out. The cohab discussion was over. Hilly had to move in with me. When she returned from Rome, she took her landlord to court, and a month later they reached a settlement. She could have all her possessions back if she agreed to be evicted for failing to pay the rent. As soon as she got her confiscated stuff out of storage, my one-bedroom apartment on the Upper West Side filled up like a thrift shop. Claustrophobia overpowered me. I couldn't breathe.

"So we'll try this for six months?" I asked.

"Sorry, no dice, this is forever," she "joked."

A month went by before we saw Dr. Selman. "So how's everything working out?" he asked when he found out we were living together. "Neither one of you has ever lived with anyone before, right?" He was right. There had been roommates, but that never quite worked out. Best friends turned into ex-friends, even enemies. "How much living space does each of you have?"

"At first I tried sleeping on the couch, then moved to the alcove above the kitchen," I said. "Hilly calls it the 'cubby.' There's only enough room for a mattress and less than four feet from there to the ceiling. If I sat up too fast in bed, I'd bump my head. So Hilly, being smaller, moved to the cubby, made it look nicer. I'm back in the bedroom."

"I moved a dresser up there, brought scented candles, hung framed pictures, and put a fur blanket on the 'floor.'"

"Why don't you two sleep together?" Dr. Selman asked.

We explained that due to our different schedules and inability to sleep with each other in the same bed, we had to sleep in separate rooms. "The truth is, it's just impossible," I said. "The last time we tried, Hilly woke me up constantly throughout the night. She doesn't snore, she sighs, and gets up to use the bathroom a lot, all of which leaves me exhausted and cranky the next day."

"We are 'incompatible sleepers,'" Hilly said. "I read about it in *GQ*. It's a common affliction, and our solution is perfectly normal and healthy. I have no problem with it, especially because George sprawls, steals covers, blankets, and kicks me, one time completely off the bed."

"Well, in that case, perhaps it's a good idea to sleep separately. Maybe even in a different zip code."

"Another issue is that Hilly wakes me up almost every morning on her way out of the apartment."

"He is an extremely light sleeper, so I'm terrified of making noise and incurring his wrath. I try to be as quiet as a mouse, and I've had to change some of my habits. Now I shower and dry my hair at night and don't make my bed or put stuff away in the morning, lest I disturb the precious angel. Oh! On my way out I leave the apartment barefoot, walk down two flights, and *then* put on my shoes."

"George, why don't you get on Hilly's schedule by going to bed at a reasonable hour and getting up together?"

"Impossible. I'm a nightlife reporter. Work schedule wouldn't permit it."

"You mean your drinking schedule?" he quipped. "Hilly, you just mentioned something about 'incurring his wrath'? Does that mean he's irritable in the morning?"

"There have been a few outbursts, but nothing too crazy. He says things like 'Please hurry up and leave! This is going to throw off my day completely! I need eight straight hours of constructive sleep, and you're driving me crazy! We can't do this anymore—we can't live together. *Get out! Go away!*'"

"She's right. The other day I threatened to take a hammer to her alarm clock if she hit the snooze one more time. She's got me waking up five to ten times before she's out the door. It's very painful."

"It doesn't really bother me because I know he doesn't even

remember saying those things, and I've heard them so many times I just laugh, inwardly. He doesn't mean what he says—it's just the irritable-male-syndrome factor. That's the real culprit."

"You know, for the first seven minutes after you wake up, you're not fully awake," Dr. Selman said. "It's like being in a drunken state."

"Should we tell him about the neighbors?" Hilly asked.

"Yes. Above us is a German girl who stomps around in her high heels all day," I said. "She may as well be digging her heels into my head. Every Sunday morning at nine a.m. she's vacuuming and stomping. Below us is a middle-aged Irish hooligan who calls himself Rat Bastard. He throws wild parties every weekend for as many as fifty college-age kids. I wait until ten thirty p.m. to call 311 and file noise complaints until the police show and break it up. Then there's the mother and daughter who have a trampoline in their backyard and invite the whole neighborhood over to jump on it. Also, the daughter is a graffiti artist. She and her hippie friends rattle spray-paint cans until five in the morning. They also have a golden retriever they sometimes leave outside. It once barked for three hours straight. I fantasized about lowering a bucket of battery acid or hamburger meat mixed with crushed glass, in order to get some peace and quiet. Only thing that stopped me was the possibility of paperwork.

"Then there's Hilly," I continued. "As much as I love Hilly, she's not helping. There's never not a noise when she's around, whether it's running water, slamming cabinets, chopping onions, sudden crashes, exhaling noisily, whistling, singing along to Bon Jovi, and the snap snap snap snap snap snap snap of her flip-flops."

"Because the sisal rug gives me little splinters that stay in there for days and they hurt," she said. "The place is such a mess I know there are mice around—Baba found one—and I'm worried they'll bite my toes. Or that I might step in cat puke. George waits for it to harden because he says it's much easier to pick it up that way."

"That sounds not only vile, George, but a health hazard," Dr. Selman proclaimed.

"The place is always a mess," Hilly continued. "Here's a partial list: stacks of old newspapers, big dust bunnies, cat hair and pubes blowing around like tumbleweeds. George flicks his used Breathe Right strips everywhere or sticks them to the walls. I found one outside on the sidewalk. He also sucks the fatty fish oil out of the gel caps, then tosses their skins on the floor. Every time I try to clean the place up, it seems to frustrate George, but then he's happy after I finish. He thanks me."

"How do you define *frustrate*?" Dr. Selman asked.

"The other night he said, 'Enough with the cleaning! I don't want to hear running water!' And then five minutes later: 'Why haven't these dishes been washed?!' But he's trying to be tolerant and patient. He just lets things build up, and then explodes."

"Is this all true, George?"

"She worries about the dishes in the sink all day, even sends e-mails about them to me."

"What's the matter with Hilly wanting to clean up?" Dr. Selman asked. "What's the matter with her wanting to keep the apartment clean? I mean, dishes in the sink? That's not even sanitary."

"It's the nonstop frantic activity. Her feet are shaking even when she's sitting on the couch. Constant noise and fidgeting makes me nervous."

"She's not fidgeting now."

"Right, but you're seeing her after work, she's in work mode, wearing a nice business outfit, and she had a glass of wine on the way over."

"You're fidgeting more than she is!" he said.

"She can't sit still during a movie. Always with the trips to the kitchen for a refill or 'I have to go to the bathroom. I can't help it, I have a small bladder!' Every ten minutes it's something! It must be the Prozac combined with white wine and neurosis. I'll stop. Maybe I'm being unreasonable here."

"Why do you think you're being unreasonable?" Dr. Selman asked, his way of confirming that.

"It's true that I'm oversensitive to noise. Maybe I have tinnitus."

"Do your ears ring?" he asked.

"No, but I hear everything ten times louder. Hilly's nervous energy is contagious and her frenzied presence rubs off on me. It might be that I'm unfit to live with someone other than a cat."

"Are you trying to say that Hilly is driving you crazy?"

"He says that all the time."

"Am I driving you crazy, Hilly?"

"No. I think it's Manhattan. Let's just find a bigger place somewhere else. In the meantime let me make things more comfortable during the time we're together."

Dr. Selman suggested I get a white-noise machine or wear earplugs.

"The other night I had my headphones on. I was transcribing an interview. Hilly crept into my office, hid behind the dresser, then jumped out and yelled, 'Boo!' I almost had a heart attack."

They laughed at me. They were still laughing at me when Dr. Selman was working our next appointment into his schedule.

* * *

New financial demons threatened. The first real sign of trouble was when Hilly refused to go to the cut-rate grocery store across the street. This emporium offered great deals such as two 2-liter Diet Cokes for $2. But Hilly found it too depressing, too noisy, "too much like Thailand." Plus it wasn't "pretty." She preferred to shop at Citarella, where they sold Diet Cokes in elegant little vintage bottles. I made reference to her princess complex. She struck back with a Little Lord Fauntleroy taunt.

Hilly originally agreed to pay half the rent. It didn't pan out. When she paid at all, she paid in installments, a third here, a fifth there. She promised to chip in for Con Ed and the phone—that is, if I gave up all the closet space. So I moved Baba's litter box out of the one by the front door. But the promise to share in utility payments didn't materialize either.

"I pay for everything," I told Dr. Selman. "From lightbulbs to Puffs Plus to extrasoft toilet paper to paper towels to—"

"I buy paper towels!" cried Hilly.

"—to dinners at Café Luxembourg. If I turn my back, she orders blueberry sorbet and champagne." Oh, we had some fine little squabbles. Mistrust was building. "I've started hiding my wallet in the apartment. If I leave it out when I take a shower or something, forty dollars goes missing."

"Twenty at the most," said Hilly.

"Why would you do that if you make more money than George?" Dr. Selman asked. Hilly explained: Part of who she was, her whole image and identity as a young woman on the go in New York City, required money. She wasn't a freshman at Miami University, she couldn't lounge around in T-shirts, sweats, and stuffed-animal slippers and order pizza.

"I don't look like this because people hand me free Gucci

shoes when I walk down the street," she said. "They don't say, 'Here's some free highlights. Would you like to get your teeth whitened, too?' I have to pay for all that! That's what girls have to do and boys don't, and it's expensive. And if you want to date that big, fat two-ton Twinkie at Rodeo Bar—"

My cell phone rang. It was my high school friend Kurtis. I put him on speakerphone. He made a public service announcement: "Hilly is the best thing that ever happened to you." Thanks, Kurtis.

That first summer, I was broke all the time. It got to the point where litter-box liners were beyond my means. Baba rebelled and used the bathtub for a latrine. Adding to the cat's annoyance was that I'd actually, in a fit of hunger, consumed some kitty breath mints Hilly had bought. We fell behind in rent.

"I don't understand," said Dr. Selman. "You lived in the apartment alone for three years and made ends meet. Why are you having trouble now when you have someone to chip in on the rent?"

"My mother's not giving me handouts anymore," I said. "And the rental-sharing concept has just resulted in both of us squandering more money. I have to fight her for the rent every month."

"The place is such a mess, it's psychologically impossible for me to invest in it," she said.

"So, you're on strike?" Dr. Selman asked. "Maybe you're looking to get evicted again?"

"Paying rent isn't an investment," I said. "It's a living expense. It's shelter, one of life's necessities. You have to pay it."

With her endearing, maddening mode of reasoning, Hilly suggested that we start looking for a two-bedroom apartment.

"So we could double our expenses?" I said.

"So I could have my own space that wasn't a disaster area."

The discussion was typical of the logic we brought to finances. For once, Dr. Selman pursued Hilly, however gingerly. She'd agreed to pay half the rent. Why wasn't she living up to her part of the bargain?

"Because I don't have any money!" she cried.

I joined the chase. "How much does your bottle of Sancerre cost every night?"

"About twenty dollars."

"So that's . . . six hundred dollars a month. I can tell you where my money goes. Last night Hilly wanted to go to Pop Burger. One hundred and fifty dollars down the drain. How many glasses of wine did you order?"

My cell phone rang again. This time it was my ninety-four-year-old grandmother. I asked her to defend me and put her on speakerphone. "George Gurley the Third is my grandson," she said. "And he's the greatest!"

Hilly executed a deft feint. "I admit I'm hopeless with money. I don't have any bookkeeping skills. I'll make a deal: why don't you manage my finances? That's the man's job, after all." It sounded like another attempt to prod me into a long-term commitment, a variation of the Joint Account Ploy. Anyway, it was a hopeless concept.

"I can't manage my own affairs," I said.

In August, the rent check bounced. Verizon Online kept turning off my Internet. November came and once again we were late on the rent. This time it was because Hilly'd had an accident. She'd given me two-thirds of her share, but then I'd done something to irritate her.

"So I removed my promise ring in protest and put it on my middle finger, where it got stuck," she said. "Later that morning, the finger turned purple so I went to the emergency room. By the way, the surgeon was really impressed with the thickness of the gold. He said it had never taken that long to saw through a gold band."

"That caper cost eight hundred and fifty dollars, which more than ate up her contribution to the rent," I said.

"Here's a moneymaking idea," Dr. Selman said. "Get married and write a book about how horrible marriage is."

That gave me an opening for raising a sensitive subject. Poverty was going to force us to stop seeing him. We simply couldn't afford the sessions anymore, even though we were only getting charged half price. I added that that was too bad because therapy had already worked wonders and we really liked Dr. Selman. His expression was a mixture of irritation, hurt, and incredulity. How could anyone use mere lack of money as an excuse to abandon mental health?

"You're going to give up going to therapy because you can't afford it?" he said.

"We just need a break until I get my next windfall," I said.

"Couldn't you forgo giving Christmas presents and put that money into treatment?" He didn't appreciate what a major thing Christmas was for Hilly. He might as well have suggested that she give up breathing. I was touched. Dr. Selman seemed genuinely distressed to be losing us. Nevertheless, we quit. It was like getting a divorce.

Two months later, we were back in his office, temporarily semisolvent. But Christmas was approaching like a rogue elephant. Hilly had been singing carols since May, and sugarplums weren't the only things dancing in her head. Unfortunately, a Moschino dress was doing a jig. Price tag: $1,800. But she claimed she could get a 60 percent discount at the sample sale.

"It would make me feel pretty, glamorous, beautiful, like a princess," she said. Of course, she couldn't pay for it herself. That's where "the boy" came in. If I loved her, I'd find a way.

But the dress was just the beginning of her wish list. A Cartier bracelet would be nice. Along with anything by Verdura or Lanvin. Surely I was aware of her fondness for rare, out-of-print jewelry books. Then for stocking stuffers: a keyboard and headphones, a scarf. Oh, she almost forgot: an engagement ring. Down the rabbit hole we went again. The way to confront our dwindling funds was to conjure up ways to spend more. I reminded her that she wasn't dating a coke-snorting investment banker from Goldman Sachs.

"I don't get million-dollar bonuses," I said. "I'm the boyfriend who has to postdate checks."

For once, Dr. Selman was on my side. "Hilly, don't you think he's being reasonable here? He can't afford these things. The dress is an unreasonable gift. It costs too much."

Hilly backed down, but set a floor. "He ought to spend at least $500."

"I'm not Scrooge," I groaned. "But see what this holiday does to people?"

Hilly was sniffling. Dr. Selman handed her a box of tissues.

"I'll do anything if you'll stop crying," I said. That made her cry more.

"What I really want is an engagement ring," she sobbed. "My family members and friends keep badgering me about why I don't have one by now. It's so depressing." She was hoping a nice present might get them off her back, alleviate her pain, and ease her mind.

"Did you know how Hilly feels about this?" said Dr. Selman.

"No, yes," I said. "I feel horrible."

"Hilly might see your lack of generosity as a withholding of affection."

Hilly sprang to my defense. "George is more than generous with me."

I was so grateful for the rescue that I leaped into the briar patch. "She wants a ring," I cried. "She really wants to get engaged. Our sixth anniversary is coming up. I get it, I get it."

"But will you really get it?" Dr. Selman asked.

I crawfished. "Can we get through the holidays first and then her birthday on January twenty-first? Can we focus on the religious aspect of Christmas?" I agreed to put more thought into presents this year.

"But will you get her the ring?" Dr. Selman persisted. Just as I suspected: they were in cahoots. Hilly perked up. She pulled out a picture of me at age seven that she'd superimposed on a portrait of Santa, driving a sleigh, smoking a pipe. She'd been investigating the ring business, she said. Visited various stores. (On the sly, I thought.) Turned out I could buy the ring without the stone and then later, when we were rich and famous, put the stone in.

"But it's up to you," she added. "You can do that whenever you want. My ideal ring is at Harry Winston and costs about sixty thousand dollars. I don't expect you to get that one, of course. And if you did, I wouldn't wear it every day. It's way too flashy. I'd be happy with something plain."

"So why don't you just give her the ring then?" said Dr. Selman.

My head spun. I felt besieged. The noose tightened. I was getting fitted for a straitjacket. Oddly, I felt excited, a little giddy. So this was where life was taking me.

For Christmas that year I gave Hilly two sweaters on sale at Ann Taylor, two books about fake jewelry, Godiva chocolates, and a candle from Diptyque. And the promise of an engagement ring. There would be backsliding before I kept that promise. But I made it. It wasn't going to go away. In a strange way, our mutual money problems were bringing us closer together. Brave new world, full steam ahead.

CHAPTER EIGHTEEN

A BITTER END, A BITTERSWEET START

Cohabitation on the Upper West Side was not working out. There wasn't enough room. I couldn't sleep; I couldn't breathe. Every other night around 3:00 a.m., I'd check into a Comfort Inn hotel around the corner. Dr. Selman suggested I go to a sleep disorder clinic, where I was diagnosed with mild sleep apnea.

When I showed him the two-page report from the sleep disorder test, he was shocked. "It looks like it took you two hours to fall asleep, and they say your blood was well oxygenated despite all of the apneas and hypopneas and whatever else. You were hardly asleep at all. You woke up sixty-three times."

"It's worse in our apartment," I said. "They told me no more booze for three hours before I go to sleep, and I have to quit smoking and lose ten pounds."

"I really think we need to move out of that apartment, and out of Manhattan. I've been looking at apartments. Unfortunately, they're slightly above our budget," Hilly said.

"Meaning in the 800,000- to 1.2-million-dollar range," I said. "At my current salary I might be able to afford that in 2032."

Money problems continued to plague us. Instead of doing the commonsense thing and pinching pennies, we succumbed to perverse, escapist logic and moved from our cramped apartment on the West Side to a luxury apartment on Roosevelt Island. Our rent doubled to $3,400 a month. Within a year, we were $8,000 behind. My mom bailed us out a couple of times, but not without expressions of annoyance and paeans to fiscal conservatism.

Every time I took my wallet out to pay for something, panic seized me. "We've got to do something!" I'd cry. That would drive Hilly into her shell. A blowup would follow, accompanied by threats of breaking up. At the same time, we were nursing delusions about a windfall. NBC was considering a sitcom based on my newspaper accounts of our trips to see Dr. Selman. Hilly and I traded rhapsodies about how we were soon going to be wallowing in money.

But one thing or another brought us back to reality. Browsing the Internet one day, I called up Gawker, where I read about a "bloodbath" at my newspaper. Six of my colleagues had been given the pink slip. "More to come," the story promised. Such is the way people learn that they've been thrown out on the street in these compassionate times. Well-wishers had added comments to the story, such as "And Gurley is still employed. Is there no justice?"

I had nurtured delusions about being bulletproof, but in a sense I'd been trying to get cashiered for some time. For several years, I'd been sunk in what I euphemistically characterized as a "slump," sometimes going for more than a month without having a story in the paper. Doom hovered at the back of my mind. A little later, I clicked Gawker again, scrolled down, and there it was—I was number seven on the list. ("I won't miss Gurley. The others, yes," another thoughtful commenter lamented.)

In a quavering voice, I broke the news. "Hillyyyyyy, I just got fired."

She handled the news with her dotty optimism. "Oh, I'm so sorry. But it's okay. It's a blessing in disguise. This is what you've been wanting. Now you're free." I admitted that I'd been pushing my luck and daring them to cut me loose by meager production. "You've handed in at least fifty e-mail resignations since I've known you, begging them to let you go," she said. "It's as if you had a premonition."

I studied her take on this. Maybe the disaster had some kind of mystical meaning along the lines of "You have to lose everything to find yourself." But I was having a hard time seeing it as a jackpot in disguise. I felt humiliated, rejected. Above all, my only regular source of income had gone up in smoke. Why hadn't I had the good sense to quit before I got fired? It would have made all the difference. If I'd handed in my resignation, it would look as if I'd gotten the best of the Man. My mojo would still be intact.

Instead, I felt like the guy in the Charles Atlas ad who gets sand thrown in his face, a pathetic wimp. I foresaw friends filing past in some kind of receiving line, offering funereal condolences. I recited the Native American saying "Today is a good day to die." But I couldn't get the hang of it. I couldn't imagine a good day to die—or get fired. I tried referring to my plight as getting "laid off." But finally I accepted it for what it was: I had been ignominiously, ruthlessly—and deservedly—shit-canned. My delusions had caught up with me. There was no refuge from truth: I needed more help from my mom. I knew it wasn't going to be easy. When I called, she was looking at fabric with her decorator. The conversation didn't go well.

"Hi, Mom, what's happening?"

"Who's this?"

"Oh, sorry, I have a mouthful of food. Eating some toasted hamburger buns with mayo and mustard."

"Wait. Let me guess. That's all you can afford?"

"Yeah, but I found some old cheese in the back of the fridge and some popcorn. That's all we have left. Hilly said I have to scrape the mold off the Kraft single first. Doesn't taste quite right. Kinda hard to get it down. Being resourceful, though!"

"That's good."

"What are you up to, Mom?"

"Not much—what do you want?"

I tried my usual ploy, tugging on her heartstrings. I'd been reduced to living on macaroni and cheese. I had to scrape all my pennies together to come up with $2.50, enough to buy a bagel, but not enough for one with extra cream cheese. But she'd heard this tune once too often. I'd dialed up a new, harder-nosed mom.

"Oh, come on, just stop, I don't want to know any more. Let's move on."

"Well, that was the good news. The bad news is I got laid off. I don't know what's going on, they may rehire me, but as far as I know, they let me go right after I asked for a raise. Guess that wasn't in the cards."

"What did they say?"

"What did they say? All right. I'll spit it out. They said, 'You're fired.' I thought a raise would be best for all concerned. I'd produce more, not less, and everybody wins. But they saw it different. They still want me to freelance for them, so there's a silver lining. The reason I was calling—besides to check in and ask how you were doing—was to see if you could help cover some of the rent this month?"

"George, I just can't do this anymore. I mean, you're forty years old. What about me? Let's talk about me. I mean, I read about this friend of yours, Clarence, the other day in your alumni magazine, and he sent his mother to St. Barts for Christmas for two weeks. This guy was in your class and he wasn't even a good student." That cut deep. She was comparing me to a onetime loser who'd struck it rich. The obvious point was that I'd turned out a failure.

"I know him," I said. "He used to try to cheat off me in Latin. He threw snowballs at bus drivers."

"I'm not saying he's a good person. I'm just saying he sent his mother to St. Barts."

"Well, what does he do for a living?"

"I don't know what he does, but I do know that he does something."

"As opposed to nothing? If I know Clarence, he's ripping off old ladies with Ponzi schemes. You ought to be proud of me for not being a crook. Instead I'm out there documenting our times for serious readers and future historians."

"*Were*, if I understood you. Listen, George. You write about strippers, barflies, playboys, degenerates—and you've become one yourself." I picked up a new tone of impatience in my mom's voice. In the past when I tried to hit her up, we'd play a cat-and-mouse game. I'd paint a graphic picture of my sufferings and the injustices of the world. She'd act coy and tease me, holding the bailout bag behind her while she made me squirm. But the money was always there. This time I wasn't so sure. For the first time, she'd hit me with a brutal truth. I wasn't prepared.

"You haven't had an article published in weeks," she said. "That's why you got fired. When is anybody going to start taking care of me, you know? I have three children. They're like vacuum cleaners, just sucking every bit of cash that comes in. Like charming, little . . . vampires."

"Mom, you live in a huge five-bedroom apartment. I live in a former women's mental hospital on what was once called Welfare Island." A desperate notion inspired me. "Here's an idea: let me move in with you."

"The guest bedrooms are taken by your two brothers, their girlfriends, their pets. We've got to figure this out. I don't know what you're going to do. Have you saved one penny?"

"Not after that bagel. The nickels and dimes went towards mac and cheese, kidney beans, Hot Pockets, cat food. I'm not eating Fancy Feast yet, but Baba's Temptation treats don't look half-bad, kind of like Chex mix, salty snacks. Think we're gonna share a meal now."

"Instead of trying to make me feel sorry for you, you need a plan."

"Hmmm, there might be some stuff around here to take to this pawnshop in Queens. Not the best neighborhood but I'll get in touch with this guy I once wrote about, Tony the Hat, now that he's out of prison. He said call anytime I needed anything. Maybe he needs an assistant." I expected her to relent, moved by my pitiful story, but she thought the pawnshop idea was a step in the right direction. I decided to try contrition.

"I get what you're saying, Mom. It's time for me to grow up, stand on my own two feet, and stop being a no-good, free-loading, bloodsucking spoiled brat."

But she wasn't through chastising me. "Then I see the movie your brother made about that horrible bar, Siberia. You're drunk in every scene, mumbling, babbling."

"That was an act. I was trying to help Jack! I introduced him to Tracy and 'that horrible bar'! Without me, no doc. Anyway, I was playing to the camera *and* working in those scenes, doing interviews. Just doing my job."

"Right, and I loved that line of yours where you say when you'd leave that hellhole, come up the steps, open the door, and you could never believe that it was actually daylight. So in other words, when I'd be at home worrying about how you're going to survive, you're getting drunk and out of control at Siberia. And then sleeping until noon or later and being out of commission for the next forty-eight hours, except to e-mail all your high school friends?"

"That's not my lifestyle anymore."

"But all those years when that was your lifestyle, I worried and supported you because I was so concerned, and now the money—now I don't have as much." Eventually, I learned that she was describing a classic case of "enabling" and that breaking the bond of dependency was the key to my own mental health, self-sufficiency, maturity—maybe survival itself.

I tried to keep the game afloat. "I see what you're saying. And now when I really do need help, this is like the boy who cried wolf?"

"The only thing the matter with that analogy is that you're not a little boy."

"I've been cutting back on expenses," I said pathetically. "No more sushi, no more seventy-five-dollar haircuts and shaves at Paul Molé."

Round and round we went. It was a replay of a replay of a replay. It went back and forth between banter and truth-telling. In a sense, we both enjoyed it because we were good at it. Years of practice had honed our skills. But it was also disruptive. My mother wasn't playing the game according to the rules.

"I understand what you're doing here," I said. "You're using tough love. And I don't blame you. But you've been telling me I have to hit rock bottom and I think I have."

"No. You're only halfway there. I've been talking to my therapist. He says I've got to stop bailing you out. It's not good for you."

I knew she was right, but I bristled. "I'm just curious. What's the long-term benefit of hitting rock bottom? I need to experience destitution and then what?"

"Then you need to face up to the reality that there is no more free lunch."

"Where'd you have lunch today? Swifty's? Le Cirque? Per Se?"

"I didn't have lunch."

"Isn't there something to be said for living in the present? Remember, you got me that book called *The Power of Now*?" I didn't tell her that I was using that guide to spiritual rebirth to prop up my bed.

"No. I'm saying you have to come to terms with not coming back to the well every time. This has been going on for years and years and years, really about twenty years. Once a man graduates from college, he's supposed to be kind of self-sufficient." Everything she said hit home. It may even have been uplifting. But it wasn't going to solve my rent problem. I asked her if I had any stock left that I might cash in.

"That's for an emergency and there's not much."

"I can't pay the rent and I'm about to eat Alpo. What's an emergency—I get evicted?"

"Getting evicted might be good for you. If you needed money for an operation, I might help you out."

I tried to rationalize my failures. "You know what happened is I got trapped, first by the idea that I was never going to have to worry about money. Then I developed this persona in journalism as a weird, unprofessional, unemployable, crazy maverick."

Mom was unimpressed. "I also don't like how you treat Hilly when you write about her."

I sensed an opening—my mother's fondness for Hilly. "Oh, I make that stuff up. On a serious note, Mom, she and I might have to call it quits. I know you love her, but it looks like I'll have to relocate to a crummy studio on Kissena Boulevard, right off Exit Twenty-Four, and she's not gonna go for that."

Silence.

"Well, that might be a deal breaker." Pause. "But you can't get along without her so you better start pounding the pavement." She changed the subject. "Did Hilly get her clothes? It was just a bunch of stuff I sent over. By the way, I understand what you're trying to do—intimidate me with the threat of breaking up. Just try to do something to make some money and let's talk in a week. I can't deal with this now. Make some kind of effort. This is pathetic. I don't care what you do, go to Gristedes and sack groceries, hand out samples of cheese, get any kind of a job. People have been in this situation before and they have found jobs."

"You're right! And I've done all kinds of things besides journalism. I've caddied at Shinnecock and Piping Rock, also washed dishes, worked in a cheese shop, had that five-dollar-an-hour construction job."

"Get a real estate license. That's what I did, at an advanced age, and I go to work every day."

"Right, good idea. While I'm looking for work, couldn't you please help me out with the rent this month? I'm supposed to be getting a freelance check any day now."

"No, this time it's *no*. Until you start working."

I gave it one last try. "Well, there is a good thing about being downwardly mobile. It forces you to appreciate simple things, like microwave popcorn. I don't need maid service, I can clean the toilet myself, and that makes a huge difference in the mood. You do a little scrubbing and then you have a clean toilet. Instant gratification. So maybe I have nothing, no security, nest egg, no hope for having a normal life, let alone a family—but I can still eat moldy Kraft singles and cat treats and derive real satisfaction and pride from that. I can savor every bite and wash it down with bug juice, still a little left. Or some Poland Spring water, none of that tap stuff, then toast up another hamburger bun. I learned how to defrost them the other day."

"That's an accomplishment? Don't you just push Defrost on your microwave for a minute and—"

"That's right, and then they're ready to go. Yeah, I can do that. I may not have enough to purchase contact lenses or enough acid-reflux medication to get me through the month. But I do have enough toothpaste and mouthwash. It could be much worse, right?"

"You could be out in the street in a box."

"That would be rock bottom?"

"Pretty close. Keep working on that."

"Here, Hilly wants to thank you for the bag of cashmere sweaters."

Hilly took the phone and started gushing about the luxurious hand-me-downs. I sat there with my antennae quivering, hoping to pick up a signal of my mother's weakening resolve, and at the same time despising myself for being such a parasite.

"Oh, thank you, thank you, thank you," Hilly said. "They were wonderful. I just pulled out one thing after another, and

today I wore the gray sweater dress and it was so great because I was so tired when I woke up, and it was there, it was
the perfect easy thing to put on, it was wonderful. . . ." After
discussing leggings, clothes, socialite party talk, Prada, and an
upcoming Sotheby's jewelry auction, Hilly passed the phone
back to me.

"George, do you want some of your stock? Think there
might be two thousand dollars left." My heart leapt. But a
string was attached. "Here's the deal. I'll help you this one
last time, but on the condition that you and Hilly join Debtors
Anonymous."

CHAPTER NINETEEN

FORGIVE US OUR DEBTS

The prospect of joining Debtors Anonymous excited me about as much as a half-eaten burrito fished from a Dumpster. I did a little research on the organization, concluded that it was another mystical twelve-step cult, and braced myself for a ration of hand-holding and mumbo jumbo. My skepticism was aroused by the notion of abundance. According to the DA line, we live in an "abundant universe." The cosmos is a safe place. If you work for it, outer darkness will provide what you need.

I found that concept hard to digest. People are getting beheaded or buried under tsunamis every day. Would they agree with the proposition that the universe is safe? It's hard to believe in abundance if cat food makes your mouth water. Lots of people work hard and end up penniless. Personally, I suspect the universe would as soon pick your pocket as pour riches on your head. Luck is as important as hard work, and blind faith sets you up for getting suckered. On the other hand, I realized that for the last twenty years I'd been a believer in abundance and a higher power—my mom. I'd gotten used to the delusion that however recklessly I lived, she'd come to the rescue.

One concept that DA pushed that did sound relevant to Hilly and me was "terminal vagueness," a euphemism for spendthrifts and people like us who are incapable or unwilling to monitor their finances. I loved that expression. It evoked an image of zombies, groping their way through life in an impenetrable fog. I couldn't imagine a better description of Hilly and me. We were vague about everything—time, purpose, compass direction, feelings. The moment we wake up, we put our vague suits on. Terminal vagueness certainly epitomized my inability to do anything definite, to make plans, to meet deadlines, to organize my life. Neither Hilly nor I kept track of our cash flow or balanced our checkbooks. We were consistently broke or in some kind of financial crisis. We never saved or thought about the future. We were compulsive shoppers. We lived on the edge, in chaos, paycheck to paycheck.

DA's weapon against terminal vagueness was "clarity and awareness." The beginning of wisdom is to develop a clear picture of how much money you have and how much you owe. Who could argue with that? It was like saying, "First, just stop being terminally vague." But how exactly do you acquire clarity and awareness?

According to one of the DA insights, we deadbeats "exult in our defects." That had a certain resonance. It reminded me of the game I played when negotiating with my mom, flaunting my screwups. Another thing that appealed to me in the DA literature was its emphasis on our culture of consumption and reckless spending and the seductive power of advertising. These bogeymen offered excuses to anyone who had a problem with prudence and frugality. Also, some of the DA literature was irrefutable stuff that offered no openings for mockery. Keep records of every cent owed, spent, earned. Make a "spending plan." Pay your bills when they're due. Don't borrow from family members or friends. I couldn't argue with that. The only thing that stood in my way was lack of discipline. I was still terminally vague about how I was going to become disciplined. First, get discipline, George. Or something like that.

The problem of the moment was paying the rent. I needed the money and my mother had laid down the law. Two trips to DA per week or no final handout. Our first meeting was held in a rec center. We entered a lobby filled with kids who'd just finished swim-team practice. It was a rowdy, festive scene, the picture of middle-class well-being—cheerful greetings, high fives, and hugs all around, kids working toward goals, parents motivating them with cheers. We felt like outcasts when we approached the desk clerk and asked in a whisper where the Debtors Anonymous meeting was to be held.

We were directed to a large, desolate room filled with metal folding chairs and card tables stacked against the walls. Hilly suddenly became self-conscious. She was carrying an alligator handbag that sold for about $18,000 and wearing a $12,000 bracelet—both items borrowed (naturally) from work.

An older woman bustled into the room and began speaking to us in a British accent before she even sat down. In a manic, nervous-cheery way, she spilled out details of her tragic, debt-ridden existence. Financial pressure had led her to "inadvertently" spend every cent she had on useless things: tea cozies, pillows, kitchen appliances she'd never use or even remove from their packaging. She had a passion for credit cards that offered "automatically approved cash advances." Now, here she was in a gloomy basement confessing to two strangers. She was well into her fifties, completely alone, a veteran of Clutterers Anonymous (for compulsive hoarders, not to be confused with Messies Anonymous). She was terrified that if DA couldn't save her, she was going to get carted off to debtors' prison.

Her mention of debtors' prison piqued my interest. I'd always thought those institutions didn't make much sense. How could you pay off your debts if you were rotting in a cell? But I suspected that the threat of debtors' prison would do more to improve my clarity and awareness than holding hands with other spendthrifts in Debtors Anonymous. Suddenly, I remembered reading that Roosevelt Island, where we were presently domiciled, was once the site of a debtors' prison—where Soapy, the vagrant in a classic O. Henry short story, longs to spend the winter but can't get himself arrested.

When the moderator entered the room, we immediately christened her the Sad Girl. Ordinary melancholy would have looked ecstatic by comparison. The look she wore was one of knowing despair. It was enough to chase any rumor of hope from the room. She was carrying some kind of a Tupperware container and a few notebooks that looked official. She glanced at us with an expression that seemed to say, "I know you two. You don't even have to tell me your pitiful story." She was nicely dressed, however, which didn't square with the long soliloquy she delivered about her pathological drive to "underearn."

When her sad tale was done, she rattled off the twelve steps of Debtors Anonymous. In short, we were powerless over debt, our lives had become unmanageable, only a power greater than ourselves could rescue us. We were exhorted to make a "moral inventory" of ourselves, to publicly admit the exact nature of our wrongs, to beseech God to remove our shortcomings, and to make amends to all the people we'd wronged. Finally, after experiencing our own spiritual awakening, we were expected to spread the message to other compulsive debtors. All in all, it was a prizewinning downer. We left the first meeting in a defiant mood.

"They're like a bunch of granola-crunching hippies trying to appear all high-and-mighty," said Hilly. "I'm not saying that because I'm in denial. I'm not hiding anything. I know what I'm doing. I just withhold financial information that I fear will incite anger . . . in you."

I stuck with my own script: God doesn't have all that much interest in the financial salvation of small-time losers. But after a little reflection, we both recognized some truth in the DA message. "Keeping one's numbers" is a metaphor for general awareness of responsibilities. "Clarity" (in our case, solvency) can purify any bad habit that pollutes your life. It can be applied to anything, from paying bills to returning phone calls to being on time. It has to do with putting away childish things and growing up. The idea of becoming an adult at age forty made me feel foolish. But the prospect of becoming a new person was exhilarating, too. And the idea of becoming adults together tickled Hilly and me. It was a project. After all, for both of us, it was long overdue. We had one secret power that would help us—the ability to have fun, even in a prosaic endeavor such as this. So despite DA's cultlike ethos, we made a pact to get what we needed out of it while modifying the rules to suit our needs. That included our practice of attending a bar before each session.

At the next meeting, when it was Hilly's turn to share, I was transfixed. Her finances were a mystery to me. I suspected at least a third of Hilly's income went to clothes. My mom had recently noted, for my ears only, that she'd never seen Hilly in the same outfit twice. Did she owe fifty, a hundred grand? I had no idea. For all I knew, she'd been a teenage kleptomaniac and done time in juvenile detention. She was usually so secretive about money matters that I expected her to be incoherent or speechless. The opposite happened. She ran off at the mouth. It was as if some dam had burst.

"My money problems began when I started working in the world of high fashion," she said. "My office at Manolo Blahnik was connected to the store, where salespeople made salaries close to three hundred K based on commissions selling shoes. The temptations and pressure to compete with them were overwhelming. I was surrounded by expensive trinkets that cast a spell over me. I wanted, needed, deserved to have them. They became necessary to my sense of well-being. If I was proud of something I'd done at work, if I'd had a fight with my boyfriend, if I'd experienced some annoyance on the subway, it triggered my shopping instinct." She always purchased her way back to equilibrium. If it was a little crisis, an $11 box of cough drops would do. A more serious upheaval might require a $150 lunch at Aquavit, or a $500 dress at Intermix.

Hilly's romance with credit cards began just before she left Manolo Blahnik. She maxed out her first credit cards at Barneys and Bergdorf's in months. When she went to work for Louis Vuitton, she got a corporate American Express card. In this particularly reckless period of her life, she spent way over her $10,000 limit. She was still paying it off years after she left the company.

"I used to come home exhausted from work," she said. "And by the time I climbed five flights of stairs I was too tired to open the mail. Besides, bills bored me. The thought of opening and reviewing the damage depressed me. Soon there were unopened stacks of bills everywhere."

It didn't take long for things to get out of control. She started asking friends for loans, $20 here, $40 there. Her parents were shocked by the news that she was living off mustard sandwiches, but they knew from past experience that if they sent her money, she'd spend it on useless things. So they sent her care packages containing such things as toilet paper and tuna, which she'd feed to the cats.

When Hilly got an offer to work closely with Donatella Versace, she quit her job. Then the Versace deal fell through. Hilly was left jobless. She had to cash in the five years of profit sharing she'd earned at Manolo Blahnik at a loss of over 50 percent because of the penalty fees.

"Stupid, stupid, stupid," she said. "But I was desperate. I applied for more credit cards and maxed them all out almost immediately. I became so accustomed to finding eviction notices on my front door, I reacted as if they were greeting cards. After six months unemployed, I finally got a job at *Newsweek*. But it paid twenty thousand dollars less than I'd been making at Louis Vuitton." She fell further and further behind. Collection agencies finally gave up on her and even stopped sending threatening letters. In a way, she won those battles. But they left her with an abysmal credit rating.

"I remember being late for work one day," she said. "When I got to the subway station, I realized I didn't have enough money on my MetroCard. I didn't have enough change in my wallet for the fare." A homeless man saw her frantically rummaging in her purse. He motioned with his own illicit MetroCard that he would swipe her through. "I was wearing the season's latest twelve-hundred-dollar boots from Chanel—and begging from a homeless man. It was strange. I didn't see the irony in that until I told a friend later on."

Still, she maintained a cavalier attitude toward spending. She expected other people to understand her priorities. A new dress or a trip to the beauty parlor came before rent. Creditors further down the ladder should be patient and wait their turn. Among the things she considers necessities are the care of her blond tresses, which she entrusts to the celebrity hairdresser Michael Murphy. He gives her a discount when he can. All the same, her once-a-month trips to Mr. Murphy cost $250 to $575. Twice a year she gets highlights for $600.

"I have the vagueness thing," she said. "I can't tell you right now exactly how much or whom I owe because I'm so successful at wiping it out of my mind. I probably have forty cents in my wallet right now, a bank balance of about negative three dollars, and some foreign currency in coins I can't exchange. And that's it. You'd think I'd learn, but I don't."

It was my turn. According to instinct, I seized the opportunity to perform, showcasing my foibles to entertain the audience and win points for laughs. In other words, to "exult in my defects." I referred to myself as a chronic debtor, slacker, and inveterate pauper. I recounted past experiences of hard times.

"In the summer of 1981, I scrounged for change in family vehicles and couches to finance my addiction to Space Invaders and Pac-Man. In 1991, I wanted to try college without classes and focused on beer, Frisbee, girls, and live music instead. I stole bacon and ground beef from my fraternity, got caught, and was shown the door. I got fired from a dishwashing job for walking off with a miniature bottle of Heinz 57. I daydream about winning the lottery and enjoy buying things with a pocketful of pennies. It's not the worst thing in the world to be broke. It can be fun." The Debtors Anonymous congregation cast stony looks at me. Not funny. Thumbs-down. I tried a more sober approach, recounting my travails with the bank in the form of a polemic against predatory lenders.

"I began digging my own grave when the bank gave me a line of credit on my debit card. They advertised it as a benign device to cover accidental overdrafts. Of course, the real reason was to dangle available credit in front of 'valued customers,' a large percentage of whom are probably like me, low-income losers. Sooner or later we suckers dip into that line of credit—'Whee! Lookee here: free money!'—and fail to keep up with the monthly payments. That means penalties, fees, and other forms of bloodletting."

I dipped into the honeypot and twice ended up owing over $3,000. I swore off credit cards for years. But after losing my wallet in Rome, I stopped by a bank branch to get a temporary ATM card. There, a sweet account lady persuaded me to get a credit card "in case of emergency"—despite hearing my whole bad-debt history with her bank. She actually tried to talk me into a $10,000 limit. I had to play the conservative, responsible adult and persuaded her to limit me to $1,400.

The card didn't budge from my wallet for a year. Patiently, it waited to be activated, whispering, "Don't forget, whenever you need me, I'm always here." During a food shortage, I finally succumbed, summoned the genie, and charged a cartful of groceries. I actually started talking to the card, thanking it for sparing me from starvation. We began a romance, my credit card and I. It was like being in love with a nymphomaniac. The card couldn't get enough of being used. Soon, I'd run up a massive debt.

For the next two years, I made monthly payments to the loan sharks while still owing them an average of $950. When a freelance check made me momentarily flush, I decided to pay off the entire balance. It wasn't as easy as I'd assumed. When I announced my noble intentions to the bank representative, a profound silence fell on the other end of the line. The rep told me I'd be charged a fee if I paid off the balance (I taped numerous phone calls with the bank representatives). It sounded like a threat. Then, I got disconnected, possibly a ploy to discourage me. On the second go-round, I reached the Automated Lady, who promised that there would be no fee. Automated Lady transferred me to another rep, who contradicted her. I would pay a fee, there was no escape.

"No wonder Americans are up to their gills in debt," I said, concluding my morality tale with an evangelical appeal. "Banks are dope pushers. They don't want us to be prudent and pay off our loans. They want to get us hooked. We are their victims." The Sad Girl, with her rueful smile, said something about "grandiose thinking" and the tendency of spendthrifts to wail about how unfairly they're treated. I felt rebuked, but justly so. Under normal circumstances, I would have shot back some sardonic rejoinder. But in the nonthreatening ambience of DA, surrounded by other misfits, I shrugged it off and considered myself from a detached perspective. I was the one who didn't mind the cash register. No one else was to blame. Perhaps I was finally able to get the picture because I wasn't going to be judged and condemned to eternal flames by my fellow sinners.

When the session was over, the six of us stood in a circle holding clammy hands, chanting, "Keep coming back! It works if you work at it!" It was exactly the kind of thing that usually made me want to gag. But I joined in like a good sport. I understood that it ran against the DA code, but I was having fun. Hilly stuck around to ask the ladies about beginners' meetings and how to get a sponsor. I waited while she exchanged numbers. She had so many questions, they almost had to push her out.

Walking through Central Park, she was on a cloud. "Oh, it was so cool! It was really, really great!"

In spite of the creepy chanting, I actually agreed with her. I admitted that I took some solace in hearing that we weren't the only fiscally challenged people in the world.

One member of the group told Hilly that she thanked her "higher power" for having made it there that night and regretted that she hadn't started thirty years ago. The Sad Girl told

Hilly that she was doing fine "so far" and gave her points for being brave. Sad Girl reminded Hilly to keep records of every cent she earned and spent every single day. Once a month, during a "pressure relief" session, all that data would be fed into a spreadsheet, which a sponsor would look over to make sure nothing was being neglected.

"There's something very basic and nurturing about this stuff," Hilly gushed on the red bus heading to our building. "The other members make me feel like they understand and empathize. They say I can fix it. In the past I've always lied to myself and other people about finances because I just felt it was easier than trying to get to the bottom of it. It's the first time I've been able to admit that stuff without feeling like the biggest loser in the world."

I, too, was amazed by her frankness. In five minutes, she'd revealed more about her financial history than I'd been able to pry out of her in the past eight years.

But suddenly she grew thoughtful. "I'm worried that if we don't follow the rules, I'll get scared away. I don't want to go home and have you grill me about what just happened. I want to play by their rules."

Now, I was a little alarmed at the radical change that seemed to have come over her. I'd noticed that psychobabble and the jargon of self-help had been creeping into her vocabulary recently. Words such as *boundaries* kept popping up. Did that mean that I was going to have to stop violating her *space*, trespassing on her feelings, trying to force her to change according to my designs?

"No, no, you do what you want," I said, trying to sound as noncontrolling as possible. "You're on your own here. Well, both of us are."

"That's why I don't want to mess it up and I'm treading

carefully because I don't want to get into these subjects without knowing enough."

I was silent for a moment. Then I tried to float a skepticism balloon. "There sure isn't much back-and-forth debate in DA meetings."

Hilly took that as a positive. "Right, it's got its own orderly structure."

"It's kinda weird because I'm so used to being able to jump in, ask questions, and steer the conversation."

"It's probably the most I've ever been able to speak without you interrupting me."

The Sad Girl hadn't made me feel defensive, but Hilly was beginning to. "Because I'm not allowed to interrupt?"

"Right. I think DA is going to have a good influence on us. It's fun because we're on neutral territory and listening to other people, and it's not even an option for us to speak."

I wasn't so sure. I felt scolded. And threatened. It looked as if DA was going to smoke me out and force me to play on a level field. I wasn't going to be able to get away with some of the manipulating ploys I used on Hilly. Was I going to have to become unselfish? Was I going to lose control?

Strangely, that prospect didn't seem so dreadful. Instead, it presented an option I'd never considered: liberation from the straitjacket of my insecurity and narcissism. It was a minor epiphany. For a moment, I felt as if I had awakened from Bottom's Dream. But I was still an ass.

Back home, we had one of the best nights since moving in together. We acted like grown-ups. I left Hilly alone to do whatever she wanted for two hours. She chose to work for twenty-five minutes and spent the rest of the time in the bathroom. Because there were no whiny complaints, outbursts, or threats ("That's it, I'm getting my own place!"), Hilly was able to relax and not worry that she might land in the doghouse. After a marathon shower, she joined me in the living room and explained how she'd just saved $30. Without interrupting, I took in all the details of Hilly's pedicure without wincing, even though one of my phobias was of exposed feet.

"First I filed my nails, then put a cuticle softener on each toe," she began. "I pushed away the dead cuticles, then put on an exfoliating scrub and massaged it into my feet, to get rid of the dead, dry skin." More details about "pumicing," self-tanning, lotion, and three varieties of nail polish followed. The point was she didn't feel rushed so it was fun for her. And what did we learn from this experience?

"Boundaries!" she said. Instead of exploding with annoyance, I discovered that I could treat her somewhat barmy dissertation as harmless amusement. After all, this was Hilly. Why not love her for what she was?

"It's funny," I said. "In the meeting, I was thinking how strange it was to be engaging in social interaction somewhere other than a bar." On cue, my cell phone buzzed. I read the message: *U out tnite? Might stop by Milady's.*

I told Hilly that I wasn't interested in another debauch. I answered the text message with a proud *Nt 2nite*. For once, I saw the obvious connection between my overspending and those nights out, which can set me back two hundred bucks, not to mention two days for the hangover and detox. Hilly gave me a Cheshire-cat smile. She'd heard these brave insights and resolutions many times before.

"Good boy," she said. "It's funny, tonight I have been drinking at a much slower pace, not with the same . . ."

"Voraciousness?"

"No, I'm just sort of enjoying it. I'm sipping rather than gulping."

"That's very interesting. I wonder if DA is a gateway to AA?"

"I hope not."

"We can fight it," I said. The one thing I wasn't ready to contemplate was giving up the bottle.

"I have to tell you," she said. "I know I bring a ton of it on myself by being irritating, but one reason I'm not guzzling is because of the lack of shouting."

I felt an argument coming on. "Really? Okay. I'll stop. Sorry. Maybe I need more self-control? And to give you more alone Hilly free time? Not always be here? What are some of the things that get me all worked up?"

"It usually starts as soon as I come home on an average workday. If you're here, you've been here all day, and my arrival triggers something in your brain, that now it's fun time. And I want to have fun. Some nights I may say to heck with it and do whatever you want. But that means, for instance, the less time I have for my feet. Really, tonight was the first time I've looked at them in six months without wanting to chop them off."

"So you'd like to spend more time with your feet and less with me?"

"I didn't mean that."

"What—do you talk to them when you're in there? Do you have conversations with them?"

"You're raising your voice."

"Of course there are ten of them, and only one of me." I thought: jilted for the sake of her toes. My cell phone buzzed. I read the message: *Come on, pussy, you're gonna miss out!* Temptation mingled with mounting irritation. Since I'd come so far in just a couple of sessions with DA, maybe I could handle this one night on the town. Besides, I needed to make a statement.

I needed to reclaim some turf. After all, I had my own space, too. On my way to Milady's, I tried to make contact with my higher power: one day at a time. And I reminded myself that each of us is the captain of three ships: partnership, friendship, and lovership.

CHAPTER TWENTY

THE ULTIMATUM

By the time of our fifty-first session with Dr. Selman, the magical powers of the promise ring had completely worn off. Hilly wanted to take matters to the next level.

"I want an engagement ring," she announced in a non-negotiable tone.

"What if George gives you the ring but without the emotional engagement that's supposed to come with it?" said Dr. Selman.

"I don't care. I want the ring. We'll cross that other bridge when we come to it."

Dr. Selman wanted to know if our living together was a matter of convenience or because we really wanted to.

"It did happen by accident," I allowed. "But I didn't hesitate for more than a few hours. I told her, I asked her to move in with me. I wanted her to. It felt like destiny. And it's working out. So far so good." I told him my plan was to see how things progressed over six-month intervals. Maybe the odds would rise as the six-month segments accumulated and eventually we'd take the plunge. Obviously I was buying time. Hilly claimed she wasn't ready either. Thinking long-term while living in a cramped one-bedroom wasn't "realistic," she said. We needed a much bigger place: two bedrooms, two bathrooms, obviously; preferably two floors.

"Maybe a wraparound terrace or a backyard for the swimming pool, tennis court, trampoline, go-cart track, and helipad?" I asked. "Or should we have all that at our country house? I figure with my current salary we might be able to afford a down payment on a two-bedroom in fifty years."

"It sounds to me like Hilly's already said yes to marriage and you're contemplating the odds," Dr. Selman told me. "So it's all up to you?"

"Well, let's see what happens," I said.

"I'm curious," said Dr. Selman to Hilly. "Do you have any problem marrying someone who makes so little money?"

"No, because I love him."

I felt a warm glow. For once, the therapy scene felt less like a rehearsal for Judgment Day. Wow, I thought. Hilly wants me even though I'm not making much more than my dishwasher wages in college. But she kept getting more militant in the months that followed.

"Get me a ring, George!" she said. "If we change our minds, I'll give it back!" She told Dr. Selman that my failure to come forth with a ring reflected my assessment of her as a loser. "Do you think I'm a loser?"

"Of course not."

"Then give me a ring." It was a beautiful example of Hilly Logic. "The other night George had a dream about proposing to me! That's a big positive step!" Hilly put a lot of stock in dreams. I'd left out the part of the dream in which the marriage proposal took place at gunpoint. At one point, Dr. Selman suggested that I ask Hilly to marry me during a therapy session.

Hilly jumped on that brilliant idea. "You're supposed to propose to me by your birthday, which is in May. But remember, it doesn't mean we have to get *married*. So just make it easier on yourself, get it out of the way, propose *now*, and don't worry. You can buy the ring without the stone and then later on . . ."

I commenced my usual evasive tactics. Then the hammer came down.

"It's December fifth," she said. "You have twenty days." It sounded like a death sentence. My thoughts turned to the relative merits of the electric chair and the gas chamber. I had one option other than running away to Mexico: the ring my father had given my mother for her engagement. This heirloom, charged with family tradition, had first belonged to my great-great-grandmother. Mom had always kept it in her safe-deposit box after the divorce with the tacit understanding that if "the day" ever came, I could reactivate it and put it back into service. Following my mom's instructions, I went through Hilly's drawers, found one of her rings, and dropped it off at Verdura on Fifth Avenue, to be *sized*. (I was learning all kinds of exciting new words.) On December 19, I picked up the ring, then called Zarela Martinez for a reservation at her eponymous restaurant, where I had been a regular for more than half my life. She promised me an opera-singing waiter who'd stop by our table to serenade my soon-to-be-fiancée.

Hilly was suspicious when I told her. It wasn't like me to plan a romantic dinner so far—three or four hours—in advance. But she agreed to meet me at seven, doubtless foreseeing some important event. When she made her grand entrance, she looked adorable. I felt strangely like a prankster experiencing stage fright. We made small talk.

"Oh, I have something for you," I said casually. What followed was a kind of parody of the gift-giving rituals that I despised so much. I didn't see the irony at the time.

"Oh, really, what's that?" said Hilly nonchalantly. I took a little box out of my jacket and set it down. When she saw VERDURA on it, she couldn't disguise her excitement. "Can I open it?" she almost screamed.

"Sure. It's nothing, really."

She opened it. A crestfallen look replaced her beaming smile as she held up a beeswax candle.

"There's something else in there," I said. Out came a little pink pig with a plastic key ring from Gracious Home. She pressed the button on the pig's head. The snout lit up and it oinked. I could see she was getting angry.

"There's something *else* in there, too."

"Are you sure?" she said, clearly getting tired of the game. Out came a pair of toe warmers. "Just what I wanted." She scrounged and found nothing. She stared at the key holder. Maybe she thought that was my idea of a ring. I decided to stop torturing her. I put the other Verdura box on the table. It had a big satin ribbon on it. She opened it up. There it was at last. Her face lit up.

"I'm so happy, so happy, so happy," she gushed. She put the ring on her finger and began blurting out expressions of love. The operatic waiter came over and tried to sing. Hilly pointed the pig at him and pressed its head. It oinked. The waiter interpreted that as a rejection and stalked away.

Then she looked at me with an expression of pure bliss. "Just think. I'm your fiancée. This has been just about the best night of my life."

The next time we saw Dr. Selman, Hilly showed off her ring. A ribbon was tied around it to hold it in place.

"It needs to be resized," she said. That was because the ring I'd used for a model was one that Hilly wore on a different finger. Dr. Selman expressed his admiration and made reference to "a dream come true." But when we told him the story about how I'd presented it, he frowned.

"So did George actually ask you to marry him?" he asked. I was fully aware that I hadn't. It was the only card I had left that would give me an out. In the excitement of the moment, Hilly had missed that detail.

"It was loud in the restaurant, mariachi music," I said. "I must have lost my concentration. But the main thing is, I still feel one-hundred-percent good about this, like I've made her happy. That's what she wanted. I did the right thing."

"The thing?" he asked. "You can't even say the word, can you?"

I was cornered. I felt like a prisoner being tortured to extract a confession. There was nothing to do but blurt it out.

"Okay. I gave Hilly an engagement ring. There it is. That thing on her finger. That's an engagement ring. We are engaged."

"Let's hear you ask me to marry you," said Hilly.

This is it, Georgie, I thought. You're at the end of the gang-plank. "Okay, okay. Hilly, will you marry me?"

She looked at me a long time and finally whispered yes.

"So everything is perfect between you two now?" Dr. Selman said.

"Pretty much," Hilly gushed. "I've been so-so-so happy. It's been lots of fun, all these people coming out of the woodwork to congratulate us, sending us champagne and other nice things. Our home life has improved. We're getting along much better."

"I think it's really great that you guys were able to make

it this far," Dr. Selman said. It sounded genuine, as if he was somewhat touched, moved, and pleased to have had a hand in getting us to the next level.

"What did you think the odds were when we first walked in your door?" I said.

"I'm not that surprised. But if you'd asked me then, I probably would have said 'No chance.'"

"I want to say that I think you've been a great therapist," I said.

He thanked me and said, "Well, we're in a new phase now. Shall we make another appointment?"

"That's right, we're all in this together," I said. "What's going to happen now?"

"That's a good question, George," he said. "Where do we go from here? It's kind of like climbing to the top of Mount Everest. Let me just point out that getting to the top of Mount Everest is only half the trip. Getting down is not necessarily easy. A lot of disasters happen on the way back."

Here was an uplifting interjection. I wondered if this was standard therapist procedure to keep happy customers coming back.

"So we were heading down the mountain?" I said. "Shouldn't we want to continue climbing higher?"

"I think the goal would be to make it down in one piece," he said.

"So what's at the bottom?"

We didn't know the answer to that one. We let it hang.

CHAPTER TWENTY-ONE

ESCAPE FROM LUNATICS ISLAND

Even though moving to Roosevelt Island had been a form of financial suicide, at first it seemed idyllic, a refuge from the chaos of Manhattan. It was so peaceful. We might as well have been in the Catskills or high up in the Alps on top of Magic Mountain. Our two-bedroom was on the sixth floor of the Octagon, a luxury building with tennis courts and a swimming pool. Right down the hallway was a fabulous gym. We had his and hers bathrooms. The apartment was equipped with a state-of-the-art washer and dryer, even a garbage disposal, a banned item in Manhattan. I enjoyed putting orange peels in ours just to watch them disappear. I spent hours looking out the window: fluffy green trees swaying above protected gardens with beautiful wildflowers and cabbage roses; children flying kites, kicking soccer balls; seagulls flying over; yachts and barges gliding by on the shimmering East River, the Fifty-Ninth Street Bridge in the distance; and above that, clouds, rainbows. It was like a nineteenth-century painting. If I held my breath, I could almost hear the hum of cars on the FDR Drive. Otherwise, near total silence.

Our concern was that Roosevelt Island might be discovered by *New York Times* readers and become the next Williamsburg or Upper West Side. Walking or bike riding around and around the two-mile-long island, I'd look "over there" and try to fathom how that teeming, cacophonous city could have been my home for three decades. I refused to venture into the pit more than twice a week because one whiff of the ammonia-scented air or a loud cell-phone jabberer was enough to trigger a panic attack. I pitied anyone who lived there, even in a Central Park West triplex.

But something about Roosevelt Island was enervating. I fell into a moral turpitude there. It was too comfortable, a hermetic mausoleum that encouraged my vegetative tendencies. I slept until noon, then spent the day chatting online with my high school friends, debating lofty issues such as Beatles versus Stones, *Star Wars* versus *Annie Hall*, and how to survive an earthquake. The highest goal of these exchanges was to win "emod" (e-mail of the day) or, better yet, "the emow" (e-mail of the week). I considered it a major accomplishment to pack up Netflix DVDs and drop them into the mailbox. Hilly would come home from a hard day's work and discover me still in my pajamas and seersucker bathrobe sipping a Bloody Mary from her Saint-Louis crystal flute. I told Dr. Selman that I was on sabbatical, in an interim stage between practicing rococo hedonism and facing the meat grinder of reality. It was only a matter of time before I'd return to wholesome living, gravitas, and hard work.

"Inability to function is a symptom of depression" was his response.

Six months later, reality did intervene. The oasis turned out to be a mirage. We fell behind in rent and the fights began. That coincided with our discovery that the Octagon was originally New York City's lunatic asylum. In the Octagon's 1849 annual report, superintendent Dr. M. H. Rahney had boasted that the "pure invigorating atmosphere" and "the most beautiful scenery" of what was then called Blackwell's Island were enough "to remove despondency, establish the health, and restore the reason." He didn't dwell on how ninety-one patients had died of cholera in an outbreak there.

Charles Dickens had paid a visit in 1842 and reported in *American Notes*, "Everything had a lounging, listless, madhouse air, which was very painful. The moping idiot, cowering down with long disheveled hair, the gibbering maniac, with his hideous laugh and pointed finger; the vacant eye, the fierce wild face, the gloomy picking of the hands and lips, and munching of the nails: there they were all, without disguise, in naked ugliness and horror."

Journalist Nellie Bly faked madness to document her experiences in our building. In *Ten Days in a Mad-House*, she called it a "human rat trap" that was "easy to get in, but once there it is impossible to get out." Those descriptions resonated with my growing despondency. That the island later became known as Welfare Island seemed like a portent of our dwindling fortunes. Returning home late one night in a cab, I was stopped by police at the entrance to the bridge. It was closed for construction. I walked across it with an aspiring songstress who was shocked to hear where I lived on Roosevelt Island.

"Oh my God, are you serious?" she said, quickening her pace as if to escape me. "I would never set foot in there. It's haunted." She made some dark reference to a fire in which a large number of women perished. I did some investigating on the Web and found that the day the Octagon opened after being abandoned for fifty years, the tram shut down, a bad omen. According to a CNN report, ghost hunters and residents have detected apparitions in the hallways. More recently, the real estate blog Curbed posted a photograph of an actual ghost on the same spiral staircase that pets refuse to walk up. Soon after watching the horror movie *Dark Water*, filmed on Roosevelt Island, Hilly and I began picking up on strange zombie emanations. Nothing spooked us more than a handwritten note on the lobby's bulletin board that read *WHY DOESN'T ANYONE IN THIS BUILDING TALK TO ANYONE ELSE?*

I told Dr. Selman of my growing disenchantment with the island. "I don't have a social life out there. If only there were a few people I could say a friendly 'What's up?' or 'Have a good one' to, even the guys in wheelchairs who smoke pot by the river."

Sensing that I was rationalizing another escapist move, he reminded me of my fantasies of returning to Lawrence, Kansas, and re-creating the trouble-free life of my college days. "A change of scenery does nothing to dispel personal demons. You'll carry them with you wherever you go until you confront them head-on."

Hilly suggested I volunteer at the hospital or get to know Gurney Man.

"Who?"

"Gurney Man," she said. "He's a really nice guy who lives on a gurney. I see him and Party in a Wheelchair every day. I'll be walking the mile to the subway and here comes Party in a Wheelchair zooming by at Mach speed. Last week I was on the tram, which was jam-packed, elbow to rib, and there was Party in a Wheelchair with his radio blasting James Brown. Then he turned it down so everyone could hear his machine that yells insults, like 'Fuck you!' and 'Eat shit!' and 'You're an asshole!'"

The prospect of striking up a friendship with these charmers did little to lift my spirits.

Hilly painted a dismal picture of me. "When I come home, George hasn't talked to anyone all day, so he's all over me and I have no time to decompress." She suggested I put a notice up on the Octagon message board.

"What, like, 'I'm lonely. Will someone please talk to me?'"

"Right! Say you work from home and you're hoping to find someone with the same schedule who might be up for some tennis or pool. Nothing wrong with that." To me, it sounded like bottom-fishing for a life.

Soon we both felt trapped. Lichens, mosses, and exotic fungi began growing on my pallid skin. I was well on the way to becoming a gibbering maniac with long, disheveled hair. Besides, the rent was eating us alive. In spite of Dr. Selman's admonitions, we began to look for a new home. It turned out to be more than a quest for four walls and a roof. It became part of the project to redesign ourselves.

We got a break when a man who worked for my mom gave us a tip. He knew about a cheap unit available in Park Slope, Brooklyn, and was tight with the landlords. Off we went seeking a new Eden. We took the subway to Brooklyn to check it out. After we got off, relying on my navigational skills, we made a wrong turn and found ourselves in a wilderness of menacing tenements. Hilly was suitably dressed for a weekend of antiquing in Locust Valley or Greenwich—quilted camel-hair jacket over pink cashmere cardigan, khaki capri pants, dainty white anklets with the Polo logo, and a flashy Hermès watch. She looked adorable and like an invitation: "Mug me."

Unerringly, I led us deeper into the projects. No other Caucasians were anywhere to be seen. And we were calling attention to ourselves by arguing loudly.

"Scoopie, I think we're going the wrong way. See that flashing sign? It says RED HOOK PHARMACY. And over there, RED

HOOK HOUSING AUTHORITY. I think that means we're in Red Hook, not Park Slope." Nor was this the fashionable section of Red Hook by the waterfront, where eco-friendly trustafarians and members of artists' collectives dwell, and the *Queen Mary 2* docks. Her logic was impeccable and the empirical evidence backed her up, but I was unwilling to admit error or forfeit my role as pathfinder.

"Those are just signs," I snapped. "I know what I'm doing. Just follow me. And stop talking. We can cut through here and go through there. I did an interview in this neighborhood a few months ago. Don't bring that map out! And don't call me Scoopie. That's just the sort of name that provokes homicidal maniacs."

But Hilly couldn't stop yammering. "Can't we walk on a nice street? We stick out like Muffy and Poopsie."

"Quiet. We'll be there in ten minutes. Keep cool. Look like we know exactly where we're going. And don't make eye contact." At the same time I was counseling sangfroid, I remembered that *Life* magazine had once designated Red Hook one of the nation's worst neighborhoods and its crack-cocaine capital.

I soldiered on. It was 3:00 p.m. on a sunny day. Conditions weren't ideal for the bloody murder of a pair of lost yuppies. Still, I was saying my prayers for the first time since childhood. We passed young men who looked as if they'd kill out of boredom. But they regarded us more out of amazement than malevolence. Maybe we looked too easy, like decoys. Maybe our country-club costumes were disguises camouflaging a pair of assassins. Or maybe they just thought we were crazy and feared that messing with us would foment some kind of voodoo retribution. Anyway, they just gawked and left us alone.

On an impulse, I made a sharp turn, hoping that we'd pop

out and find ourselves in some middle-class, white-bread sanctuary. Instead, it was a cul-de-sac. Back we went. A change seemed to have come over the neighborhood. Young men in white tank tops and baggy pants were everywhere. They zoomed past on BMX bikes. They walked scary, fang-baring dogs on flimsy-looking leashes. I thought I heard one of them say, "If I was ever going to kill a motherfucker, it would be right now."

"Walk faster," I hissed. "Don't show fear. They can read that in our body language and facial expressions." I tried to affect insouciance while my nervous system was twisted into knots. Up ahead, some kind of communist demonstration was in progress. I marched faster. Hilly fell behind. Against my express wishes, she asked for directions. Three enormous ladies outlined an intricate way out of the labyrinth.

We retraced our steps. Now we passed crazed-looking men giving us the evil eye. Muscular youths stopped shooting hoops and stared at us. A man appeared with a pit bull frothing at the mouth, lunging at its chain. "She won't bite," he said with a sinister grin. We followed a sinuous street for a couple of blocks, made a few turns, and suddenly emerged into a tidy, quaint, gentrified neighborhood.

"Are you mad at me?"

"No!"

We walked in silence for a half hour until arriving at our destination. Hilly was turned off at the outset by the chain-link fence and a BEWARE OF THE DOG sign. The owner had to open three locks to let us in. The door itself was protected by steel bars. The apartment looked as if it were designed for dwarfs—two cramped rooms, low ceilings, small kitchen, tiny bathroom, bars on windows in the back, no natural sunlight, minimal closet space.

Even though Park Slope had been named one of America's ten best neighborhoods, Hilly and I were both emotionally stuck in Manhattan-centric snobbism. Brooklyn—just the name itself—seemed like a step down. She was uneasy about the forty-five-minute commute she'd have to endure twice a day. I envisioned her disturbing my sleep every morning at the crack of dawn. We thanked the owner and fled, determined to find lodging where people of our stature belonged, on the Island of Bloated Illusions.

The first apartment we considered was a shoe-box one-bedroom on a busy stretch of East Sixty-Fifth Street, with soundproof windows, two functioning fireplaces, and an elevator. It was surrounded by chic boutiques, French bistros, one block from Central Park. After the broker called us "shoo-ins," we had lunch across the street at La Goulue, frequented by rich society types—just the sort who'd warm up to "our kind."

Hilly was bubbling. "Incredible," she cried. "Paradise." She gushed about the invisible hand of destiny and how wonderful our future was going to be. This magical apartment was going to change our lives. Somehow, it was going to help us get our finances in order. In her patented ditzy logic, Sixty-Fifth Street would enable her to learn how to play the piano because Steinway was just a few blocks away. Now she could get the Scottie dog she'd always dreamed of because the apartment was close enough to her office that if the pup had problems, she could dash home and minister to it. We'd forgotten to ask about laundry, but that was no problem because "people just do it for you" in nice places like that. For various reasons, the apartment repelled me from the moment I saw it. But I couldn't bear to smother Hilly's enthusiasm, so I played along, nodding, smiling.

"So we're going to be real fixtures around here?" I asked.

"Yes! I'm going to be glamorous, skinny, and beautiful. People at work will be groaning about the long commute to Brooklyn Heights, and I'll be, like, 'Bye, bye. I live right around the corner. I'm walking home.' Just think, we'll be living near the Gutfreunds, Anne Bass, Kitty Carlisle Hart, Mike Wallace, Ace Greenberg, Ivana Trump, Jayne Wrightsman."

"And the Bernie Madoffs. Maybe we can be their DA sponsors!"

She ignored that and kept rolling. "And when people ask if we still live on Roosevelt Island, I'll say, 'No, we live on Sixty-Fifth Street.' 'Oh, really, where?' 'Between Fifth and Madison, closer to Fifth. . . . Yes, there's a fireplace. . . . Of course it works!'" She wasn't finished. "Scoopie, someone's really looking out for us because all our prayers have been answered. It's quiet for you, two separate rooms, and we're practically going to be forced to be interesting because just between office and home there will be so many opportunities for encountering interesting people. We'll bump into people we know and get invited to parties: 'Hello, Richard Johnson? Yes, of course we'll go to that event with you. Look, there's Kenny Jay Lane and Mary McFadden. Yoo-hoo! Big kiss!'"

My mom, a realist and a real estate broker, agreed to take a look at the dream abode the next day. It took her about five seconds to douse it under a bucket of cold water.

"Too small," she said with grim finality.

"Too small, too expensive," I said. "Also, way too many Euro-trashy sleazeballs with weird names like Nico and Sophocles, wearing pressed blue jeans, loafers, watches, and ludicrous jet-setters lounging about in their suede jackets. 'Oooh, it's so chilly in March, I'd die without my suede jacket and this lilac sweater wrapped on my shoulders. Are you coming to Gstaad with us? Oh, you must!' 'I would but I already have plans to go to St. Barts on Sasha's private plane. We're staying with Carlos, who has a beautiful villa there, and everyone's so attractive, even the natives, and that's the only thing that really matters—besides money.' 'That's right, there's an inherently moral quality about money and being attractive. Look out, don't step on the homeless person!' Yechhh. Sorry, Hilly. But the East Sixties really give me the willies. I should know, I grew up there. Right across the street from the married guy in *The Seven Year Itch*."

Our next stop was a one-bedroom on East Fifty-Third Street. The feng shui outside the second-floor window was cars exiting the FDR Drive and screaming their way to First Avenue. We'd be living at the intersection of chaos and bedlam. I asked Mom and Hilly to leave me alone in the bedroom. I sat on the floor, closed my eyes, and tried to imagine our first night there. Thirty seconds wouldn't go by without a bus whooshing past, a cabdriver honking, a car alarm screeching. I'd wake up to those sounds at 5:00 a.m. It would be impossible to sleep without a hammer and a Demerol IV drip to keep me knocked out. How did I know? Self-awareness and from having lived in seventeen similar residences—from Spring to Sackett Street to East Tenth, Seventeenth, Thirty-Eighth, the Sixties, Seventies, and Nineties, to the West Sixties, Seventies, Eighties—all over New York City. I staggered into the other room.

"Hilly? Sorry, I'd crack up here."

"What if I found some soundproofing solutions?" she chirped. "One good thing is the proximity—"

"To Bellevue, the cracker factory? And to your office ten blocks away?"

"No, Scoops, to the river. You can walk or ride your bike along it."

"Or jump in it? Sorry, not gonna happen." I eyeballed the agent. "Anything else in the building without the pandemonium amenity?"

On the way out, Mom said she'd called the little old lady who rejected our application for the ground floor of a Brooklyn Heights town house, demanding an explanation. I had a pretty good idea it was a combination of Hilly's credit and either my salary or my thought-provoking articles on sex, drunkenness, and politics. Mom had tried without success to arouse empathy by asking her if she had kids of her own, or a beating heart.

"You know, I actually like getting rejected," I said.

"Don't tell me that," Mom said.

"No, really. It makes me feel special, like an outlaw, like society can't control or tame me."

"Maybe you ought to give conformity and normalcy a try," said Mom. "Like go to bed before five a.m. and get up before noon."

"Or wear matching socks," Hilly added. "Not to mention shoes sometimes. Or celebrate holidays, or sing 'Happy Birthday' or make plans, or permit people to say 'Bless you' when you sneeze, or get happy because it's sunny out. Or go to brunch, attend a wedding. Or see a movie with a gerund and a name in the title. He refused to see *Raising Helen*."

"That's right, Mom. I think movies like *Surviving Picasso, Killing Zoe, Serving Sara, Becoming Colette, Finding Forrester, Chasing Amy, Being John Malkovich, Educating Rita, Eating Raoul, Saving Silverman, Saving Private Ryan, Teaching Mrs. Tingle,* and *Wrestling Ernest Hemingway* should be outlawed."

"You didn't like *Being John Malkovich?* There really is something wrong with you, George," my mother declared. They were ganging up on me again.

"All the things Hilly just said are evidence of a maverick spirit," I said. "I stand for independence in thought and action." Silence. At lunch I retaliated by teasing Hilly about the time she got evicted. The two of them looked at me with death-ray glares, the same reception I got at Mom's dinner parties when I'd claim that Hilly has at least five drinks a night and a tiny butterfly tattoo above her bottom.

"Sorry, I just like getting everything out in the open and having a sense of humor about things," I said. "It's very AA."

"No, you're being provocative and disrespectful," Mom said.

Next stop: a one-bedroom way east on Seventy-Sixth Street. It was only $600 less than our current rent. I had a vision of us by the end of the summer: flat broke, stuck in a new, overpriced prison, losing my mind. Hilly had private thoughts, too. Twenty blocks was too far to walk to work and she hated the 6 train. She'd run into people she knew at the gym. Mom said she was willing to cosign the lease and pay for a wall to create a second bedroom in the living room.

In the grim, shabby lobby, the broker gave us an application. Her look suggested she'd already rejected us. She seemed too preoccupied with herself, too busy on her BlackBerry. When she mentioned a routine credit-rating check, I knew it was curtains. Mom was innocent of Hilly's past troubles in that department, so I thought it best to take her aside and explain. When Hilly joined us, Mom lightly scolded her for not mentioning or dealing with her credit history. By the end of the block Hilly was sobbing, I was apologizing, trying in vain to mediate and absorb some blame. She felt betrayed.

We were having a drink after a DA meeting in the same neighborhood when I abruptly said, "Let's not live here." I had written about that area before and described it as a wasteland, crowded with sports-lounge restaurants, hair salons with names like Vanilla, a Dunkin' Donuts and Le Pain Quotidien on every block.

Shaking off her sense of betrayal, Hilly agreed, "It would drive me to drink and debt. There's something about the pace that isn't quite right. I couldn't walk around here comfortably. It's too uptight and fake. People are mean to waiters. I'd feel as if everyone was judging me for things that are beyond my control." Now, we were back on the same page. But she was still upset about the episode with my mother. I tried to argue that since Mom was going to cosign the lease, she needed to know about the credit issues.

"It's just that I felt ambushed," Hilly said.

"I should have cleared it with you first. I could have found a better time to open that can of worms. You're right, it wasn't fair. After all, my credit rating is as bad as yours."

"Well, we'll see what happens in seventy-two hours when my skin breaks out all over my body as a result of the stress I went through. But it's okay. It all worked out."

Later, when we reviewed this scene for Dr. Selman, Hilly spilled out her hurt. "George changed his mind about Sixty-Fifth Street right after his mom saw it. I was gone for maybe ninety seconds getting some iced tea, and when I came back, it was like he'd been hypnotized. Right before, he said it was going to be 'perfect.' Then he said he didn't think it was 'quite right' for us. And then he just went on a tirade dumping on it. It was so bizarre and I got so angry!"

"That was Method acting," I explained. "Make-believe. I pretended to be someone excited about living there and didn't like the character I became. And so I told the truth."

"What you need is to learn how to tell the truth without violating the trust," Dr. Selman said.

I had a comforting sense of our ironing things out, rather

than having a shouting match. Hilly had summoned a little humor. And I had recognized my own contribution to the discord. We'd both taken a baby step in the direction of problem solving. We were learning to come to each other's rescue.

Of course, the harmony was short-lived. The next evening we had a spectacular brawl. When I came home late and opened the door, I felt totally disoriented. In my absence, Hilly had plunged into one of her manic redecoration frenzies. Her mother's advice for dealing with men included the axiom that occasionally you have to "rearrange the furniture." Mrs. Heard had meant this metaphorically—you have to shake things up from time to time, to throw the man off-balance and reassert your powers. But Hilly took it literally.

So periodically she'd summon a superhuman energy and undertake another incomprehensible rearrangement of the furniture. It looked as if a cyclone had hit. The furniture had flown around the room and settled in odd corners. Two couches, three chairs, and an eight-foot-tall bookcase had been moved to new locations. The TV was now facing south, the rug lay kitty-corner to its former position. My carefully littered possessions had been hidden away in various drawers. It was like the work of poltergeists. Vertigo seized me. Then outrage.

I heard the television in Hilly's room. When I burst in, she hid under the covers. I mastered my anger and left her alone. Opening the refrigerator, I found a squish toy representing George W. Bush dressed in a sombrero wearing an Emiliano Zapata mustache accompanied by notes in Spanglish: *¡Hola amigo! ¡Dubya quiere ayudarle a hacer el chile!* I understood that this bit of tomfoolery was calculated to divert my inevitable anger and pressure me into lightening up. It also showed that she knew she'd committed a heinous crime and was in serious trouble. I reverted to my Damien personality and let a tantrum build.

Just then I spotted an envelope poking out from under the front door. Something about it was dangerous looking. Definitely not a two-for-one deal on slices of pizza. I tore it open. Sure enough. It was our latest rent statement, along with a lawyer's letter threatening eviction if the balance wasn't paid at once. The deficit had grown to $7,000—twice what we'd been expecting. That meant Hilly had failed to pay the $4,000 she owed, which she'd promised to take care of a month before.

I flew back into her room in a fury and woke her up. She rubbed her eyes dreamily and said it was all wrong. It didn't reflect the actual amount we owed. She'd already talked to the building manager about it. I reminded her that the same thing had happened four or five times while we'd been lost in terminal vagueness on Roosevelt Island.

"Did you pay the four thousand?" I asked, clenching my teeth.

"No," she said sweetly. "But I will. I don't know what happened. Some kind of snafu with my paycheck."

I was levitating by now, lifted off the floor by righteous indignation. "All right!" I bellowed. "That's it. I'm moving to Kansas. My life here feels over."

"Don't be so dramatic. You shouldn't make any rash decisions." She sounded exactly like my mother in her "mommy" voice, which infuriated me even more.

"Look, it's over," I cried, slipping into infant mode. "If I don't get out of this now and hit the road, I'm finished." I retreated to my room and sulked. A half hour later, there was a muted knock on the door.

"What?" I snarled. Hilly had made scrambled eggs and bacon for me. It smelled pretty good. I went into the living room and sat down. "I'm going to Park Slope this afternoon," I said after a long silence, with a mouthful of eggs. "I'm going to talk to the landlords about that place we saw." Pause. "I'm moving there with or without you."

"I'll come with you, Scoopie," she said brightly. Wonderful girl. Lovable, lifesaving girl. You are too good. I don't deserve you.

"Okay," I said.

CHAPTER TWENTY-TWO

SECOND COMING

Off we went to Brooklyn to take a second look at the place that had seemed like such an ill-fated dump on the first go-round. What a difference a little change in mood or perspective can make. Dispirited by our Manhattan search, we saw the Park Slope pad in a new light. We overlooked the chipped paint on the ceiling and the nonfunctioning fireplace and pronounced it a chic pied-à-terre. Hilly forgot about the long commute and launched into one of her rhapsodies.

"I love this neighborhood," she said. "There's a toy store and two wine shops right on our block." What the toy store offered was unclear, but I easily grasped the significance of the two wine shops nearby. It meant no more evenings without a bottle of Sancerre. We shook hands with the landlords, sealed the deal, and celebrated in one of the convenient bars. A glass of wine fired Hilly up even more. Park Slope was going to be our Shangri-la. We were going to save so much money we'd be able to afford a trip to Hawaii that Christmas. Moreover, the new apartment was going to transform us into responsible adults.

"We'll pool our resources like normal couples do," she said. "We'll start making investments. And we'll be totally honest with each other. If one day we want to get a Scottie dog or have a baby—people do that, you know, like there are hundred-year-old women in Korea who are giving birth to healthy babies. . . . I think we're doing the right thing."

I apologized for the blowup the night before. "I guess sometimes I need to blow up to clear my head."

"I know. You're a drama queen."

I let it go. We were feeling too amped and buzzed to bicker. As usual, the euphoria didn't last long. The exodus from Roosevelt Island was choppy. We didn't schedule the move properly with the Octagon, and the building manager forbade us to do any moving outside our allotted four-hour slot. The day before, I began smuggling our possessions out one suitcase at a time, emptying the contents in the back of a van, then returning for more. Sneaking away from Lunatics Island felt like a jailbreak.

From day one, Park Slope was bliss, a revelation. What had we been thinking before this move? I'd been living for years as a transient person in Manhattan. My living quarters had ranged from a $30-a-night, fleabag welfare hotel where I peed in the sink to avoid the mental patients waiting in line for the bathroom to Mom's beaux arts, Parisian-style town house on the Upper East Side.

While I enjoyed the high and low life, I never felt completely at home. Without knowing it I was always trying to get out of Manhattan. I was beginning to feel that the city itself was a demon that had corrupted and depressed me, in spite of Dr. Selman's refutations of this line of thinking.

Park Slope seemed like the home we'd both been seeking. Suddenly, we could afford a basic existence. We felt rejuvenated. Hope and optimism shone down. Now we could afford to go to restaurants, movies, join the YMCA. Or spend $100 at the grocery store, purchase a portable air conditioner, an enormous wardrobe closet, a "waterfall" fountain. We temporarily suspended our DA frugality and forgot various homilies and mantras about minding money and balancing budgets.

But it wasn't the reckless spending that invigorated us as much as savoring the pure air and relaxed pace. Obnoxious cell-phone talkers, in-your-face nut jobs, aggressive flyer distributors, and other parasites hadn't discovered Park Slope. Neither had the stereotypes we'd been warned about, such as the status-seeking, double-wide-stroller-pushing moms and their henpecked, castrated "alterna-dad" spouses. When Hilly reported spotting a bespectacled, bearded father teaching his daughter the lyrics to "Helter Skelter," I assured her they were North Slope interlopers. She and I stayed within a ten-block radius in the less-gentrified outskirts of the South Slope, which also meant fewer trendy hot spots and young hipsters.

We did experience a moment of alarm when a Jordanian family opened the Hookah Lounge and Head Shop on our street. But in spite of offers such as the "Buy One Get Two Free" bong sale, we never saw a single customer enter the place (and were thrilled when it was shuttered months later). Our landlords, George and Mimi, brought us plates of chicken curry, rather than eviction threats, and constantly inquired about our happiness. We helped carry their grocery bags up the stairs and paid the rent on the first of the month, if not before. Mimi took care of Baba when we were out of town. We actually had social interactions with our neighbors— unthinkable in Manhattan.

Even our occasional disputes seemed to improve and become more civilized in Park Slope. Typical tiff:

"You're blowing things out of proportion."

"I don't care!"

"Well, I do."

"Talk about double standards!"

"You're yelling."

"I've tried all kinds of other voices and nothing else works."

"You haven't tried speaking in a normal tone of voice."

"You're driving me crazy."

"It seems as if every single thing I do drives you crazy," Hilly said. "You're pretty much the only person who thinks I'm irritating. Except a couple of glossy-mag editors. And my mother."

Such arguments were now ending in laughter and a couple of beers as we listened to ourselves playing the worn old tapes. And they often resulted in flurries of apologetic e-mails the following day.

"Now I feel guilty. I love you. Is everything okay?"

"Oh, Scoopie, I love you, too. Everything's okay."

We saw a lot of our new neighbor Ipah, who'd once worked for my mom as a cook and housekeeper and had prophetically christened me Number One Fool in my teenage years. As a sign of my growing sense of responsibility, I took Ipah's dreadlocked, geriatric cat to the vet for her first checkup in well over a decade. It was a challenge. Katie wailed, scratched, and hid under furniture. Finally I covered the twenty-eight-pounder with a towel and crammed her in her crate. Halfway to the animal hospital, Katie broke free. I chased her down the sidewalk, imagining the look on Ipah's face when I reported that her beloved cat had been run over. I managed to corner her and got her back into the cage, but not without serious lacerations and loss of blood.

The doctor put Katie under for grooming and seven teeth

extractions. The next day, when I picked her up, she seemed much friendlier. Eventually she stopped hissing and waddling away whenever I offered her Temptations treats. She purred, let me brush her with Baba's FURminator. She even permitted me to cradle and rock her. Taking care of Katie made me feel that I was emerging from a dark age of self-absorption. I dared to fantasize that I might be evolving into a human being capable of compassion, of doing things for others. The glow of sainthood suffused my brain. It was a little startling to think all it took was the move to Park Slope to bring about this transformation.

Then Katie got sick and refused to eat, which required more doctor visits. Twice a day for five weeks I force-fed her steroids, appetite stimulants, and painkillers and never gave up, until she gave me a "No, you're back, please kill me now" look. Eighteen hundred dollars later the vet said there was nothing left to do. It was time for Katie to leave this vale of tears. I was stroking her during the sedation but couldn't stay for the fatal overdose. When I gave Ipah the bad news over the phone, we both cried. I kept the ashes and gave her the clay mold of dear Katie's paw print.

Now I felt like a kitty killer. Over and over, Hilly swore I wasn't responsible for Katie's death. In an effort to keep the halo of sainthood, I visited Kusnah, Mom's other longtime ex-housekeeper, in a nearby nursing home. I brought her a plant, framed photos, a scented candle, and fifty bucks. Otherwise Hilly and I kept to ourselves, receiving only occasional visitors, who never stayed more than an hour. The three times we went to a local bar, we were home by midnight.

CHAPTER TWENTY-THREE

WHO ARE YOU?

We hadn't seen Dr. Selman for twelve months. It was time for a reunion and progress report. We told him about our adventures in Debtors Anonymous, about the move from Roosevelt Island, about my getting fired. After a brief updating, I unburdened myself of guilt feelings from our second trip to Rome together.

Hilly took me along for her company's anniversary gala, which she'd worked on nonstop for nearly a year. But instead of being supportive, I'd been a jerk, treating it as a nuisance that interfered with my own demands for entertainment and attention.

"He's been going way overboard about this," Hilly told Dr. Selman. "But I think it shows how much he's changed, how introspective he's become. He can step outside of himself now and see where he's at fault. I don't come home to Furious George anymore. He doesn't give way to anger as much and blame the world for his problems. It's really helped our relationship."

"This project was very important to Hilly," I persisted. "And I resented it for taking time away from me. Then when I saw what she'd actually accomplished and met people from her company who praised her, it just hit me what a selfish jackass I'd been. Any normal person would have encouraged her for those ten months and backed off when she needed to work. Not me. It was 'Oh, God, do we really have to talk about that now? Sorry, I don't speak that language, can't deal with this jewelry and decorative arts talk.'"

"You're being too hard on yourself," she countered. "Sure, you had your moments, but that's human nature. The fact that you realize all this stuff is fantastic and something to be proud of. And you're not selfish." We could almost have gotten into an argument over it.

"When she was working on the project, there was always some crisis, some insurmountable problem that turned out to be a tempest in a teapot," I said. "So after a while, anytime she talked about work, I thought, here we go again, little girl crying 'Wolf!' Now she's going to whine and bawl and wring her hands. What I failed to realize was that I behaved the same way over my crises with the newspaper."

"Stop beating up on yourself," she said.

Dr. Selman listened with a faint smile. I think he was mildly amused at the knack we'd developed for self-analysis. I told him about one recent night when I was indulging in one of my bouts of self-flagellation, begging Hilly to forgive me for various real and imaginary misdeeds and indiscretions when she held up her hands.

"Stop! Wait!" she said. "Now I have something to apologize for." That jerked me out of confessional mode and unleashed dreadful suspicions. Had she watched an episode of *Friday Night Lights* on the sly? Had she begun to dabble again in witchcraft? Did she steal my credit card and charge $5,000 at Gracious Home? Or did she have an affair circa 2004 and is she having one now with the George upstairs? I could handle all that, I decided. No problem.

"It's okay whatever you did," I said. "Really, I deserve what's coming." But what if she was going to announce that we'd come as far as we could together and that it was time to break up?

"I'm going to watch *Law & Order* right now," she said.

"You do that every night. What is it that you have to apologize for?"

"What I'm apologizing for is that I'd rather watch my show right now than listen to you apologize to me."

"So she shut you up," said Dr. Selman. "She asserted some independence. And you didn't throw a tantrum. You took it like a man. Bravo. I'm impressed. That is progress."

We attributed progress to our practice of holding fairly regular one-on-one therapy sessions with each other—over dinner, in bed, on walks, in buses and trains. I'd been taping our little fights, and after DA meetings we'd go out for drinks and evaluate our performances. Then we'd try to figure out what we had learned.

"I owe Hilly at least five years of deference," I said. "That's approximately the length of time she's put up with my misbehaviors and mistreatments." According to my self-imposed rehab program, I now gave in to her on all matters. If she wanted to go to the Mexican restaurant, I'd ignore my gastroenterologist's warnings about spicy food, cheese, onions, garlic, and beans. If something happened to Hilly at work, I'd listen to the details with a rapt look on my face. I took care to close kitchen cabinets, to stop dropping ashes on plates, to do the dishes, and keep the toilet seat and lid down at all times. I wallowed in apologies for failures of empathy and various transgressions. I praised her cooking, even when she served up a burnt offering.

"When I come home from work, he calls out, 'I love you, Hilly!' Rather than growling or saying, 'I want a hot dinner now followed by bam-bam.' Every time he goes to the store, he comes back with a treat for me. He's so thoughtful it's almost suspicious."

"She looks at me as if she's not sure I'm George. She gets up close and scrutinizes me and says, 'Who are you?'"

We talked about our new utopia. "Park Slope really makes Manhattan seem like the lower depths," Hilly said.

"As soon as I get off the subway in Manhattan, I smell urine," I said. "I'm happy to be here now, for an hour, but can't wait to go home." Manhattan used to inspire manic bursts of energy. I now associated it with corruption, chaos, dissolution, skanky bars, and sleazy clubs filled with vultures, killers, sadists, succubae, parasites, excess, folly, obsessions with status, party lists, and begging for table-scrap quotes from celebrities.

Twenty years before, when I was attending Kansas University, I'd met William Burroughs and heard him say, "You don't need the vampire, the vampire needs you." That pearl of wisdom expressed what Manhattan had become to me—a bloodsucking fiend. Now, if I needed a "humanity bath," I'd go to the deli, the library, the Botanical Gardens.

Back when Paul Sevigny was starting out as a deejay, I wrote a kind, sympathetic profile, which gave me carte blanche when his bar, the Beatrice, opened. But after it became the most exclusive watering hole in New York City, Mr. Sevigny shunned publicity and asked that I not write about it. Needing the money, I'd ignored his request and wrote my personal guide to the Beatrice. As soon as the piece was published, I was banned.

Eight months later, he said he'd lift the ban if I showed up dressed as a clown. A few nights later, I appeared outside the Beatrice at midnight wearing a Technicolor French clown suit, clown shoes, orange Afro wig, Coke-bottle glasses, makeup. The doorman let me in and I danced around for four hours, a rubber chicken in one hand, a horn in the other, to get back into the fold. In my new Park Slope personality, I couldn't identify with the fool in the clown suit. "Who are you?" I asked. Although still retiring as late as 5:00 a.m. and rising just before noon, I was a morning person in spirit now. I befriended our elderly neighbor who sat by her window all day keeping a stern, watchful eye on everyone. It pleased me to mouth, "Hi, Rosa," and receive a smile or wave. Boring had become the new exciting. Visiting the aquarium in Coney Island sounded better than a new nightclub. Somehow I easily managed to elude friends who continued to torment me with texts and e-mails: *Hi love, what r u up to? . . . Whatcha doin? U out? U coming later? U up 2 anything tnite? . . . Don't be late I'm hungry yo. Maybe meet up early at Katz? . . . Miss you xoxo.*

"Who are you?" Hilly said after she saw me exchange pleasantries with the Vietnamese couple who ran the Laundromat or the cashiers at the lesbian coffee shop. She felt as if I'd been put under a spell.

"George and I both have stubborn, sometimes rigid personalities," said Hilly. "We're finding that by taking things slowly, we're less likely to let little disagreements explode into major battles. I don't feel I have to walk on eggshells around him as much anymore."

"No more threats of ending the relationship?" Dr. Selman asked.

"Nope!" But I admitted there had been a few minor flare-ups. "I blew a fuse after Hilly moved the surge protector to the corner of the living room, then insisted on cleaning the blinds so I could breathe better. But if we'd still been on Roosevelt Island, I would have pummeled her with insults and accused her of destroying my mood. And I'm no longer checking into hotels in the middle of the night, saying I can't breathe, like I did on the Upper West Side. So, not as much melodrama and a lot more levity. Not being up to our armpits in debt has made it easier to coexist."

"So Damien doesn't have the upper hand anymore?"

"I used to get so upset and frustrated and angry about so many things," I said. "I'd just shut down and be unable to communicate with anybody."

"Now he's able to rein in his anger," said Hilly. "Because you have all this extra space and you don't have these vampires sucking the lifeblood out of you."

"Damien's still in the background," I said. "But as long as I limit his access to alcohol, he keeps quiet." Dr. Selman took that as a sign that I was on the right road. Becoming jobless had something to do with it, I said.

"He didn't like feeling controlled and manipulated," said Hilly.

We had another little disagreement over that. "No, the pressure was inspiring. I needed a fire lit under my ass."

"And having your mind messed with all the time?" she asked.

"That was lighthearted. I may have exaggerated the hazing. Besides, I was a real handful and pretty much asked for it."

"They used to give him 'gay edits,'" Hilly said. "Meaning they'd edit his articles in order to make him look really, really gay."

"I asked for that, too. Hey, it was my idea to interview a hundred New Yorkers and ask what percentage gay they were.

In the article I confessed to being six percent gay because I talk in a high-pitched voice and like Joni Mitchell a lot."

Dr. Selman laughed. He wasn't one to encourage victimhood, but he agreed that leaving the newspaper, even by the extremity of getting fired, might have been good for me. I'd been there thirteen years. I'd gotten into a rut. Somehow I'd approached the job as a mandate to cultivate a persona of excess and self-destruction.

"I wonder if you miss that image," he said to Hilly.

"That was George when we first met and started going out," she said. "From the beginning he made it clear that our relationship would have to have boundaries, one of which was his freedom to 'party,' which he defined as drinking himself under the table once a week. We had fun out together, but when the clock struck twelve, I'd go home and he'd stay out."

"And you were happy to let George put you in a cab?" asked Dr. Selman.

"Right. And let him keep on raging. Also, I didn't want him to associate me with that world, the dark side that takes place in the wee hours when people are really loaded. Recently, I looked at our e-mails from the first year. Even back then he reported that it took him several days to get the toxins out of his mind and body after a night of bingeing. It seems pretty dysfunctional when we talk about it now."

That got us back to the subject of booze. I told him that drinking had lost some of its charms recently. My mother had warned that as I got older, it wouldn't be as easy to come down and bounce back. She made some dark warnings about genetic factors that might predispose me to addiction. So I'd begun to wonder whether seven to ten hours of self-medicated, illusory rapture was worth seventy-two hours of resulting agony.

I decided to follow my gastroenterologist's "lifestyle change" advice and added a few rules. No more than three drinks a day. No nightclubs. Park Slope bars were okay so long as I didn't become a regular. It worked. No more hangovers or therapeutic eating binges. I lost five to ten pounds. My acid-reflux attacks were cut in half. After a decade of taking proton pump inhibitors (Nexium, AcipHex, Zegerid) twice daily along with Pepcid AC and Zantac, I quit everything cold turkey except Perrier, saltines, the wedge pillow, and the occasional Alka-Seltzer.

I also tried to impress Dr. Selman with my current reading list: *Codependent No More; The Irritable Male Syndrome; Relationships for Dummies; The Complete Idiot's Guide to a Healthy Relationship; Liver Detox Plan; I'm Dysfunctional, You're Dysfunctional; Republican Gomorrah;* and *Responsible Drinking*. I told him that I was considering attending AA or "moderation management" meetings.

CHAPTER TWENTY-FOUR

DR. SELMAN EXONERATED—
AND DEIFIED

We'd covered a lot of territory with Dr. Selman over the years: sex, anger, alcohol. Name any contemporary neurosis— we had our personal, original version of it. Sometimes we left his office in rapture, sometimes in the slough of despond. But we were always ready to talk. In fact, we ran off at the mouth. It was as if we'd just emerged from a monastery and were breaking a vow of silence. We couldn't stop the flow of confessional blather.

Our relationship with him had gone up and down over the years. At times we felt frustrated by his aloofness and the sense that we weren't getting to the bottom of anything. At one point I'd suspected him of wanting to sabotage our relationship so he could steal Hilly away from me. During other paranoid spells, I worried about his zeal for prescribing medications. I even imagined getting a restraining order signed by him, a straitjacket, and a one-way ticket to the sanitarium.

At times he seemed annoyed with me for introducing subjects such as my longing for an adult-size Big Wheel. In one session, he announced that he was "bored."

Sometimes our sessions were more like social occasions than hard-core therapy. He, Hilly, and I had actually hung out a few times. Once, after therapy, he invited us to his bachelor pad. He opened a bottle of wine and we shot some pool. (He beat me three games in a row.) Another time, we bumped into him at Elaine's, made some small talk, and traded jests. We met his daughters. It was as if we'd become friends more than patients.

Before our first trip to Rome, he'd given us recommendations for restaurants and "a good bar." This seemed odd given our alcohol issues. Was he encouraging us to drink? He also asked if we could do him a favor. There was this article of clothing . . . He gave directions: exit the Hotel Eden, make a left, go in the direction of the Via Veneto, walk up a little hill, and enter a men's shop that sells black cashmere scarves for 115 euros. Could we pick one out for him? He'd pay us back of course. This, too, seemed odd, the kind of favor you'd ask mentally healthy friends to do, rather than a couple of basket cases who were paying you to shrink their heads. Was there some psychological subtext? We never knew.

Over time, as Hilly and I began showing a few signs of personal growth, I reevaluated my reservations about Dr. Selman. At the beginning, when he pushed the drug approach to therapy, I suspected that all he had to offer were pharmaceuticals or that he was getting kickbacks from the industry. But it occurred to me that maybe he'd given up on me as a candidate for self-directed change, since I rejected so much of his advice, and concluded that drugs were the only hope.

It had bothered us the way Dr. Selman sometimes allowed

our sessions to meander. He reminded me of a Latin teacher we could derail from a grammar exercise by asking him about the design of the Roman javelin or the travesty of the Dodgers' move to the West Coast. Once I got Dr. Selman off the track by asking him about my cock-blocking duels with Ptolemy. He indulged me and admitted that he was a big fan of Howard Stern, who often addressed the subject. There were three motives for cock-blocking, according to the Selman Hypothesis:

"One, the cock-blocker wants the woman for himself. Two, he wants the man for himself or sees the woman as a threat to his relationship with the man. Three, it's an expression of hostility toward one or both of the parties."

I suggested that the sport between Ptolemy and me fell into a different category of cock-blocking. "Couldn't it be a game, a kind of bonding device?" I said, explaining that Ptolemy and I were friends. "We have debates about whether a true friend should always act as a wingman. Friends sometimes cock-block for laughs and sometimes to protect each other."

"All right, if you want to prevent your friend from making a mistake, it could be a good thing."

"Yes, that's another possibility."

"Knowing you, though, I'd say it's one of the top three things I mentioned. It's because you like the woman or you like the man or it's sort of like a free-floating hostility."

We flogged the subject for quite some time. It was more like a bull session than a therapeutic probe. I asked him if I should abandon cock-blocking.

"I'm not going to tell you how to behave," he said. "I wouldn't go out looking for women with a man who I know is going to cock-block me. I'd be pissed. If I was hitting on some woman in a bar, and somebody tried to cock-block me, if I was

seriously hitting on her, if I was really on the make and looking to pick up this particular person—and you came in and
cock-blocked me? I'd be fucking pissed."

I enjoyed the bull session, but it was hard to imagine Freud
delivering a tirade like that.

"But isn't it all war?" I persisted. "Men compete for women.
Isn't that what keeps us alive?"

"But the thing is, you're an engaged man now. So what do
you have to gain? It's not war for you. The war is over. You're
a noncombatant, a civilian. You should be generous. To give
is better than to receive, you see, and to give is better than to
cock-block."

These digressions were amusing, and ostensibly pointless.
But maybe we were revealing buried truths about ourselves
in these rambles, and maybe Dr. Selman gave us rein because
we were coughing up useful insights. To be fair, he was also an
expert at steering things back to relevancy and our would-be
goals. Whatever was going on behind his mask, we couldn't
deny that he'd opened us up. He acted more like a midwife or
a referee than a didactic lawgiver and, in effect, goaded Hilly
and me to diagnose ourselves.

Eventually, my skepticism about the Selman approach to
therapy turned into a born-again belief in him. Because Hilly
and I had undergone so many positive changes since we made
our first visit to him, I credited him with being a wizard.
Simply going to see him kept us focused on what we had to
change. In his office, we learned to become comfortable talking about subjects that had been taboo and painful. Early on,
I wondered if Dr. Selman's presence was superfluous and if
we couldn't have achieved the same results if we'd done our
talking in front of Baba or Hilly's stuffed sea lion, Scruffy, for
an hour. But back then I was terminally vague and woefully
myopic.

One more thing about Dr. Selman—he was a superb listener. He listened and he remembered, and on more than a few occasions he consummately pulled all the threads together. Maybe that's all you need in a shrink. And when we veered into outer space, he eventually reeled us back in. While his straightforward, sometimes blunt, and clinical persona wasn't always warm and fuzzy, he never smothered us with avuncular bromides or New Age psychobabble either. I kept trying to get him to declare his bedrock principles, but he was evasive. I suppose it would be like a magician giving away his tricks. When I asked him about the relevance of Freud to couples therapy, he parried with his own question: "Do you think of me as a latter-day Freud?" When I pointed out that he had a picture of Freud on his office wall, he executed another dodge: "Freud had an interesting life." It was maddening.

"What do you think Freud would have made of Hilly and me?" I said.

"Probably the same thing I make of you," he replied. "But you're changing the subject, digressing." I wanted to ask him what he thought of Andrew Salter's quip that psychoanalysis was like "trying to nail lemon meringue to a wall," but decided against it. That would be digressing, too. I did get one provocative Freud comment out of him: "Freud would probably say that because Hilly treats you like a child, you're really having sex with your mother."

Whenever I claimed to have changed my self-destructive behavior, he was like a courtroom lawyer: "Where's the evidence?" Once he threw up his hands in frustration and declared, "You two are complete opposites. She gives you all these emotional massages, and if she's vacuuming or bothering you in some little way, you threaten to jump out the window."

I tried to convince him that I was actually a person of sensitive feelings. "I cried during an episode of *The Love Boat* once after a scene with a young Michael J. Fox."

Hilly came to my defense with her own analysis of my psychological quirks. "You know what I think it is? From the moment he was born, George has always been a kind, wonderful soul. But he just got a little bit confused when he was a kid and his parents got divorced. He wasn't really sure what was going on or who he was. It upset his whole understanding of relationships and people being together and families and stuff. He wanted to belong to a family, but he felt insecure, like an outsider around the new families his mom and dad formed. He once told me that going back and forth between the two families made him feel like the pebble in a shell game."

In Hilly's view, I'd learned to play the role of the court jester, trying to win laughs for approval and acceptance. I sought out friends who were misfits, "outsiders" like me who tried to compensate for a sense of alienation by outrageous behavior. I saw the newspaper as a kind of alternative family and tried to get too much from it—love and validation instead of just a salary.

"Anyway, now you're free," she said. "You have a chance to be yourself." It was a mouthful and I saw some glimmer of truth in her analysis. But what struck me was how articulate and persuasive Hilly sounded. She stayed focused and didn't go round and round, chasing stray ideas. Dr. Selman gave her a pat on the back.

I followed her monologue with a report on our love life, which had improved since I'd become liberated from gainful employment and since we'd moved to Park Slope. For the second time in eight years, I'd said those three little magic words during carnal relations. Like an old-fashioned Victorian guy, I even began referring to the sex act as "lovemaking." Interestingly, Hilly persisted in calling it "getting dirty" and "bam-bam." On Roosevelt Island, we'd been distant. Sex there may as well have taken place in our separate bedrooms. Now there was eye contact with the lights on or dimmed, not pitch-black. Long, meaningful, pointless hugs before and after, too, the kind I'd seen happy married couples do. Now when the deed was done, I was the one who called for a bit of cuddling and "after-play," while she begged off so she could take a shower or watch the *Law & Order* spin-off about sex crimes.

CHAPTER TWENTY-FIVE

ET IN ARCADIA NOS?

It is a glorious day in Park Slope, as is every day. Nary a cloud has appeared in the sky here since the Battle of Brooklyn. . . . Ripe fruit falls from the trees. The songbirds serenade us with Puccini arias. Ponce de León was just looking in the wrong place. The Fountain of Youth is right here, just down the block from where we live. Come on over anytime and shed ten, twenty years.

We've got it good in Park Slope. But like good Americans, we want *more*. Hilly dreams of being an arbiter of taste in the fashion business. She wants to be her own boss, keep her own hours, answer to no one, have a department created for her, rule over a staff of lackeys, have lunch at La Grenouille every day, go to fancy dinner parties, and get a lot of free stuff. The beach bar in Hawaii still beckons, but it's on hold.

She requires two Scottie dogs to complete her happiness, along with a new straight nose. She dreams of medical miracles that would make it possible to have children without nine months of pregnancy. Her wish list also specifies a car and

driver, an inexhaustible supply of Cartier cigarettes, *Law &
Order: SVU* on twenty-four hours a day, self-folding sweaters,
and world peace.

Myself? I just want to have a new pair of tube socks every
day. Hilly, I want to thank you. I'm a different person, thanks
to you. And if I occasionally succumb to an outburst of anger,
it's only because I'm *pissed off.* Isn't everyone? Don't we have a
right to be?

My tempters are still busy: *Cocktails soon? . . . Hey what's up,
stranger? Where are you? Surely you're not working tonight. Martini? . . . Wanna help organize a pill crawl? Are you going to Sa-
mantha's store opening? . . . Dude! Do it! You got a weed number?
Let me know when you're up for some pool.*

Let you know? How about I let you know I don't like to be
told to let you know? In fact, let me let you know right now I
will never let you know whether I'm up for some pool—and if
you let me know that you want me to let you know one more
time, I'll never let you know anything ever again.

That's pretty much the end of our little tale. We're here,
wrapped up in our cozy cocoon, celebrating life together in
quiet ecstasy. Things are moving at a frightening full speed
ahead. My mother called and said, "There's going to be a
wedding this summer." I said, "Whose?" She said, "Yours."
I overheard Hilly the other day talking to her gynecologist
about childbirth considerations for a woman her age. She and
I are going out tonight—to our first AA meeting. Our minds
are open. We know all about change. Of course, we'll probably
stop somewhere for a drink before we go.

ACKNOWLEDGMENTS

To my father, George Gurley Jr., who helped edit this book and my mother, Katherine Bryan, who also helped make it (and everything else) possible; Dr. Harold Selman (still putting up with us after six years); Marthann and John Heard; Susan Gurley; our siblings (Austin, Alexis, Arianrhod, Ashley, Cern, Gill, Jack, and Jonathan); and Baba.

Observer legends Peter Stevenson, Peter Kaplan, and Jim Windolf; super-agents Ed Victor and William Clark; everyone at Gallery Books, especially Jennifer Bergstrom, Tricia Boczkowski, Jeremie Ruby-Strauss, and Emilia Pisani. Also: Sarah Sper and Patrick Price. A special shoutout to my grandmother Agnes "Gimma" Gurley and to Sarah Dunn, Hilary Shor, Hampton Stevens, Henry Phyfe, and the rest of The Group (Todd Fogarty, Bruce Owen, Kurtis Bell, Paul Wagenseil, Andrew Preusse, Luc Lafontan).

As well as: Tracy Westmoreland, Chris Wilson, Sarie Calkins, Paul Hawryluk, David Patrick Columbia, Joanna Corson, Jeanine Pepler, Tiffany Dubin, and hundreds more, among them Dr. Stephen Lamm, Jacqui Lefton, Alexandra and Sven Adame, Michael Thomas, Lauren Ramsby, Susan Morrison, John Homans, Bruce Mason Angissima . . . all the Ptolemys and Ingas we've ever known . . . Bill Flaherty, Vicki Waller . . . Desmond, Ron "Captain Nirvana" Hesler, Ipah, Erie, Kusnah . . . Baroness Sheri de Borchgrave . . . and to my first literary co-conspirator and spiritual adviser: C. S. Ledbetter the Third.